SHARING THE RISK

SHARING THE RISK

How the Nation's Businesses, Homes and Autos Are Insured

JAMES R. MARKS
Project Director

JOHN D. CRAIGIE
Vice President-Publications

INSURANCE INFORMATION INSTITUTE
110 William Street
New York, N.Y. 10038
(212) 669-9200

$5.95

First Edition—March, 1981

Library of Congress Cataloging in Publication Data

Marks, James R., 1956-
Sharing the Risk: How the Nation's Businesses, Homes and Autos are Insured.

Includes index.
1. Insurance [Casualty] 2. Insurance [Property]
I. Title. II. Title: How the nation's businesses, homes and autos are insured.
1981 81-65769
ISBN 0-87491-519-8
ISBN 0-87491-520-1 [pbk.]

Design and Art by Dorothy Fall
Printing by Colortone Press

PREFACE

Property and casualty insurance in its many forms touches the life of virtually every American. It provides financial protection for home owners and renters, car owners, business owners and their employees—even for people who suffer personal injuries or property damage at the hands of others.

Because of its significant role in keeping the nation's economy moving and in serving as a source of financial security for individuals and their families, property/casualty insurance has become a major topic of attention among members of the news media, consumer leaders and educators.

Nevertheless, many people don't understand how insurance works. What their policies cover. How companies price their products, and where the money goes. How the insurance business is regulated. How the business relates to our society as a whole. The purpose of this book is to provide understandable answers to these questions, and others.

"*Sharing the Risk*" was prepared to help people who want to acquire a better overall understanding of the property/casualty insurance business—representatives of the news media, consumer leaders, educators, students, new employees in the business, and any buyer of insurance who would like to know more about the product.

This book was prepared by James R. Marks of the staff of Insurance Information Institute, under the supervision of John D. Craigie, the Institute's vice president—publications, and with the able assistance of other staff members who served as writers, reviewers, or both.

We also had the benefit of a technical review by Norman Hoffman, assistant professor, The College of Insurance, and of an editorial analysis and review by J. Carroll Bateman, associate professor, College of Communications, University of Tennessee and former president of the Insurance Information Institute. Their contributions are deeply appreciated.

We also acknowledge with our thanks the assistance of a number of experts whose reviews of certain sections of the book have helped to assure us of a better finished product: William G. Clark, senior vice president, General Reinsurance Corporation; John F. Donahue, CPCU, assistant vice president, The Hartford Insurance Group; John R. Eklund, director of marketing development, The Hartford Steam Boiler Inspection and Insurance Company; Richard I. Fein, senior actuary, National Council of Compensation Insurers; John E. Hart, CPA, partner, Coopers & Lybrand; Walter M. Kramer, vice president, American Institute of Marine Underwriters; Gerard J. Nolan, CPCU, president, Parkington Associates, former president, New York State Excess and Surplus Lines Association; and Lloyd Provost, general manager, The Surety Association of America.

The Insurance Information Institute was established in 1960 to improve public understanding of the property/casualty insurance business and to report to its member companies trends in consumer opinion affecting the business. In publishing this guide for the lay person covering all aspects of property/casualty insurance, the Institute adds a new dimension to its publications program. Other major publications of the Institute include the annual *Insurance Facts* book, *The Journal of Insurance*, *The Executive Letter* for member companies, *Overview* for regulators and legislators, plus a variety of special reports, research studies and consumer guides.

We welcome your comments and suggestions.

Mechlin Moore

Mechlin D. Moore
President
Insurance Information Institute

CONTENTS

APPENDIX

AN INTRODUCTION TO INSURANCE

GROWTH AND ROLE OF INSURANCE

Thousands of years have elapsed since a group of Chinese merchants devised an ingenious way of protecting themselves against the chance of a financially ruinous upset in the treacherous river rapids along their trade routes.

They simply divided their cargoes among several boats.

Now if one of the boats was battered to pieces in the rapids, no merchant lost all of his goods. Each stood to lose only a small portion.

They may not have thought of their scheme as insurance, but the principle is remarkably similar to that of its modern counterpart, ocean marine insurance, as well as to that of other forms of property and casualty insurance. Reduced to simple terms, insurance is a means of minimizing the losses of a few by spreading the cost among many.

The folly of people *not* taking steps to safeguard their investments was made plain when some 14,000 buildings were destroyed and 200,000 persons left homeless in a fire which raged through London in 1666. The first fire insurance company was founded in London the following year.

FIRST U.S. FIRE INSURER

In the New World, the first fire insurance firm was formed in 1735 but lasted a scant five years. It was Benjamin Franklin who got fire insurance off to its real start—in 1752—with the successful formation of the Philadelphia Contributionship for the Insurance of Houses from Loss by Fire (also known as the Hand in Hand). That company is still in existence.

Property and casualty insurance has come a long way since those early days.

When the automobile came along, insurance wasn't far behind—to provide financial protection and peace of mind to car owners whose accidents, though few in those days, nevertheless could be costly. What is said to be the first auto liability policy written—actually a policy for horse-drawn carriages made applicable to an automobile—was issued in 1887 to one Gilbert Loomis of Westfield, Conn. The cost was $7.50 per $1,000 of liability coverage. Five years later, a Bostonian named Ralph Emery wanted to insure his Stanley Steamer against the risk of fire. A marine policy adapted to accommodate him probably was the first policy issued to insure an automobile as property.

FIRST AUTO POLICY

Over the years, property/casualty insurers have expanded their horizons to provide coverage against almost all known perils, ranging from fire to the violence of hurricanes, tornadoes, and earthquakes . . . to the actions of white collar and other criminals . . . to the consequences of one person's negligence resulting in harm to another.

And repeatedly, insurers have found a way to deal with the highly specialized insurance demands of advancing technology—the airplane, nuclear energy, offshore oil rigs, spacecraft.

Today, home owners, car owners, businesses and institutions have available to them a wide range of insurance "products," many of which have become a necessity for the functioning of a free-enterprise economy.

The companies that provide those products constitute one of the nation's most competitive, but closely regulated, industries. The intensity of the competition is reflected by the fact that of the more than 2,800 property/casualty companies, no single company or group of companies with common ownership has more than 7.5 per cent of the market. The ten largest companies combined can claim only a little more than a third of the market.

DEGREE OF COMPETITION

Many of the largest companies operate in every state and sell just about every form of property/casualty insurance. Others serve more localized markets, operating in selected states or even in a single state.

A measure of the economic significance of the insurance industry is the ratio of the total annual premium income to the nation's gross national product. In the United States, total insurance premiums (including life insurance) represent more than 7.5 per cent of the GNP—a ratio which is considerably higher than that of any other nation. The property/casualty segment alone exceeds 5 per cent, which is higher than the total premium-GNP ratio in all but a few nations.

Property/casualty companies in the United States provide employment for close to 500,000 persons, not counting the more than 600,000 agents, brokers and service personnel who represent the business in other capacities.

FUNCTIONS OF PROPERTY/CASUALTY INSURANCE

Our society could hardly function without insurance. There would be so much uncertainty, so much exposure to sudden, unexpected and possibly catastrophic loss, that it would be difficult for anyone to plan with confidence for the future. Most importantly, it would be difficult to obtain credit or financing since few lenders or investors would be willing to risk funds without a guarantee of safety for their investments.

Technically, the basic function of property/casualty insurance is described as the transfer of risk. Its aim is to reduce financial uncertainty and make accidental loss manageable. It does this by substituting payment of a small, known fee—an insurance premium—to a professional insurer in exchange for the assumption of the risk of a large loss, and a promise to pay in the event of such a loss.

SPREADING RISK

Transfer of risk also is referred to as "spreading the risk," because the large losses of a few are distributed through an insurer to a large number of premium payers, each of whom pays a relatively small amount. The larger the number of premium payers the more accurately insurers are able to estimate probable losses and thus calculate the amount of premium to be collected from each participant. As loss incidence may change, insurers are in a constant process of collecting loss "experience" as a basis for periodic reviews of premium needs.

As an additional benefit of insurance to society, insurers themselves, as the trustees of policyholder and stockholder funds, become major investors and suppliers of capital to the economy. In this respect, insurers perform a capital formation function similar to that of banks. Thus, business enterprises obtain a double benefit from insurance—they are enabled to operate by transferring potentially crippling risk, and they also may obtain capital funds from insurers. Consumers benefit through the availability of a multitude of products and services, and the economy from the hundreds of thousands of jobs created within the insurance industry and in insurance-related occupations.

Consider the economic impact of the private insurance industry in one state alone, New York. Throughout the state in 1979, insurance companies—both property/casualty and life—employed more than 162,000 persons on an annual payroll of over $2 billion. These companies contributed more than $200 million in corporate taxes and their employees paid some $90 million in sales and income taxes.

THE INSURANCE PRODUCT

The insurance product is a contract, known as a policy, which legally binds the seller (the insurer) and the buyer (the policyholder) to certain obligations. Insurers are obligated to pay for losses should a specific event covered by the policy occur; policyholders are obligated to pay a premium for the financial protection provided by the policy.

KINDS OF PROTECTION

Property/casualty insurance companies offer a wide range of products (policies) covering:

- losses of or damage to property resulting from fire, windstorm, theft, vandalism and many other perils;
- the policyholder's legal liability to pay for injuries to other persons or damage to their property for which the policyholder is responsible;
- costs arising from job-related injuries and illnesses;
- protection for employers against losses caused by fraudulent or dishonest acts of employees (offered in the form of fidelity bonds);
- the failure of a contractor to perform specified acts within a stated period (suretyship).

A major difference between a property/casualty insurance policy and other products is that the tangible benefits of the insurance policy are realized only after some kind of loss has occurred. Insurance is a promise to pay in the event of a loss *in the future*. But it is important also to remember that those policyholders who do not suffer a loss benefit from financial protection every minute of every day.

Property/casualty insurers today are prepared to provide coverage against almost any predictable kind of loss. To be able to do this, they find it essential to keep in close touch with the changing needs and demands of the modern marketplace.

The "package" policies which home owners and businesses

take for granted today, for example, were an outgrowth in the 1950's of a perception by insurance companies of the public's failure to protect itself adequately against certain potentially disastrous financial losses. Prior to that time a majority of persons purchased limited insurance coverage (such as fire and windstorm only). Many did not carry liability insurance, and thus left themselves open to severe financial losses which could grow out of lawsuits.

INSURANCE "PACKAGES"

Today's "package" policies combine liability coverages and a wide range of property coverages—all at a lower cost than if the coverages were purchased separately.

Other products, not used as widely, are equally important to those who need them. With the renaissance of the nation's cities, people living in good quality older homes often found it difficult to get the standard homeowners package because of the prohibitive cost of repairing or replacing their homes with materials of a quality equal to the original.

A policy form that was developed in the 1970's provides such property owners with broad-based protection calling for replacement of damaged portions with construction materials that are in common use today—the old hand-plastered walls in a burned out room might be replaced with wall board, for example.

The energy crisis, with its attendant increase in the cost of gasoline, has spawned such innovations as policy endorsements to protect participants in carpools, and specific forms of insurance for vanpools.

Innovations in insurance to meet changing situations extend far beyond those involving individuals. Consider the risks peculiar to the nuclear power industry, for example. Insurers have developed a complete portfolio of coverages for such risks to allow for the orderly growth of new energy sources.

MAJOR POLICY PROVISIONS

The property/casualty insurance industry has a large variety of policies and coverages which are, in some respects, as individual as each policyholder. Nevertheless, there are characteristics common to most policies.

POLICY ELEMENTS

The typical insurance policy comprises four sections:

- The declarations page—names the policyholder, describes the property or the liability to be insured and states the type of coverage and the maximum dollar limit that the insurer will pay in the event of a claim;

- The insuring agreement—describes the insurer's and the policyholder's responsibilities during the time the policy is in force;
- The conditions of the policy—spells out details regarding the coverage and what is required of the insured and the insurer in the event of a loss resulting in a claim;
- The exclusions—details the types of property and the types of losses that are not covered.

Included in the conditions section are provisions common to many property/casualty policies. Among them:

COMMON CONDITIONS

- Concealment, fraud. Should the policyholder in any way willfully conceal or misrepresent any facts or circumstances in applying for the policy or in the filing of a claim, the insurer may void the policy and refuse to pay any loss.
- Perils not included. Most property insurance policies exclude losses caused, directly or indirectly, by certain perils including enemy attack, rebellion and civil war. Coverage of certain damages may be denied if they result from a policyholder's failure to use all reasonable means to save and preserve property during or after a loss.
- Waiver provisions. Essentially, any changes or modifications of the policy terms must be written and attached in the form of an endorsement to the policy. Oral or separately written changes cannot alter the policy terms.
- Cancellation. A policy usually may be canceled by the policyholder at any time or by the insurer under certain conditions. The remainder of the premium will be returned on a pro rata basis if the policy is canceled by the insurer. A charge for administrative costs will be made if the policy is canceled by the policyholder.
- Mortgagee interest and obligations. Since some property covered under the policy may be mortgaged, the lender has a vested interest in the insurance on the property. Under this clause, the insurer recognizes the lender's interest.
- Pro rata contribution. This provides that if more than one policy is in force for the same property, each company will pay a share of any loss in proportion to the amount of coverage it agreed to provide. This effectively prevents an unscrupulous policyholder from over-insuring his or her property in order to profit from a loss.
- Requirements in case of a loss. Among the policyholder's

responsibilities are: prompt notification to the company; protection of damaged property from further loss; submission of proof of loss, and making available at the request of the insurer all pertinent financial records.

- Appraisal. Should the policyholder and the insurer disagree on the value or the amount of a loss, this provision outlines the procedures for selecting and paying independent, competent appraisers to arbitrate and determine a settlement.
- Company's options. This allows the insurer to take all or part of the damaged property at an agreed value after payment, or to repair, rebuild or replace it with material or goods of a similar kind and quality, or to settle in cash.
- Subrogation. The insurer, after paying a claim to a policyholder, has the right to recover the amount of the payment from a third party who either caused or was responsible for the loss. Consequently, the policyholder waives his or her right to collect twice—once from the insurer and once from the third party.

DEDUCTIBLES

Many insurance policies—covering homes, automobiles and businesses—include provisions for "deductibles."

Under these provisions, the policyholder agrees to absorb losses up to a certain amount—the deductible. By offering deductibles, insurance companies are able to reduce the cost of the policies because they are relieved of the obligation of handling a multitude of relatively small claims—those less than the deductible amount—which occur in great numbers and often cost just as much as large claims to process. Among commercial insureds, who often "retain"—or self-insure—substantial portions of their risks, deductibles are also commonly known as retentions.

COST REDUCTION AID

Where it is economically feasible, insurers urge policyholders to increase the size of their deductibles as a means of holding their premiums to a minimum.

PROPERTY INSURANCE

Anyone who owns property has an insurable interest in that property. The purpose of property insurance is to provide owners with financial protection against the loss of or damage to their property because of fire, windstorm, theft, vandalism or a host of other perils.

Property insurance policies do not necessarily cover all property owned by the insured. A policy covering a family's home and personal possessions does not apply to such properties as automobiles and large boats, for example. Each policy spells out what is covered.

The policy also lists the perils against which the property is protected as well as certain perils which are not covered. A home owner can buy a policy covering his or her dwelling against fire and lightning only, or a special homeowners policy offering financial protection against a wide range of perils. ''All-risk'' policies cover losses caused by all perils except those which are specifically excluded.

"ALL-RISK" POLICIES

Property insurance is sometimes referred to as ''first-party'' insurance because it covers only the property owned by the policyholder, or the first party to the policy contract. (The second party to the contract is the insurance company.) On the other hand, liability insurance (see below) is often called ''third-party'' insurance because it is designed essentially to protect the policyholder against losses of other persons (third parties) for which the policyholder is legally liable.

LIABILITY INSURANCE

Liability insurance pays for property damage or bodily injury losses the policyholder may cause to others. Its roots trace back to ancient concepts of retribution and it was developed further in English common law under the principle of torts. A tort is a wrongful act, resulting in injury or damage, on which a civil action may be based.

Liability insurance differs from other insurance coverages because of its relationship to the law.

DETERMINING FAULT

Since liability losses involve a third party, a determination of fault or responsibility must be made—sometimes in the courts. The impact that court decisions can have on insurance is exemplified by what has happened in the field of medical malpractice liability. This was a relatively stable segment of insurance until the mid-70's when changes in legal concepts by courts widened the potential for successful malpractice suits. Because of an increase in liability suits and awards, malpractice insurance claims payments began to exceed premiums, resulting in large losses to insurers. This was reflected later in higher malpractice insurance premiums, or by the reluctance of some insurers to issue policies. There was also an increased demand for coverage by medical professionals who suddenly recognized their vulnerability to suits which could ruin them financially.

Umbrella Liability

Although the liability insurance which most people carry will meet the individual policyholder's needs in a wide variety of circumstances, the amount of money it will pay is limited to the amount stipulated in the policy. Also, there are some situations, such as libel and slander, which a standard liability policy does not cover. However, special policies are available for such protection.

PERSONAL CATASTROPHE PROTECTION

To enable people to protect themselves against catastrophic lawsuits in such situations, insurers offer a special form of coverage known as umbrella liability.

Umbrella liability insurance gives the policyholder excess coverage (up to $1 million and more over and above that provided in other policies) as well as primary coverages in some other instances.

Umbrella liability coverage has come to be in high demand among individuals who have substantial assets and who therefore may be especially vulnerable to lawsuits and costly judgments.

PERSONAL LINES

AUTO INSURANCE

More than 25 million auto accidents a year generate a heavy casualty toll—some 50,000 deaths and upwards of 5 million injuries—as well as economic losses which inflation pushes to new heights each year. $10.2 billion in 1960. $23.5 billion in 1970. $56.4 billion in 1979. $100 billion, in all likelihood, sometime during the eighties.

LARGEST INSURANCE LINE

It's little wonder that auto insurance is far and away the largest single property/casualty form of coverage. Of every ten dollars that Americans spend for property and casualty coverages, four go to pay the premiums for insuring motor vehicles.

With most car owners today, the cost of auto insurance has become an essential item in the family budget—a safeguard against the prospect of an accident the cost of which could range from the inconvenient to the catastrophic.

Indeed, lawmakers across the country have taken steps to require that drivers are prepared to provide compensation (usually through insurance) to *innocent victims of accidents* for which those drivers are responsible. They have done so through enactment:

- in many states, of laws requiring all registered car owners to carry insurance (or, in a few cases, to post some other form of security) to pay for potential injuries to others or damage to other people's property.

FINANCIAL RESPONSIBILITY LAWS

- in every state, of laws under which a driver involved in an accident may lose the right to drive if he or she is unable to provide proof of financial responsibility up to certain dollar amounts.

Some states have so-called comparative negligence laws which limit the amount a person injured in an accident may recover in a lawsuit in proportion to the percentage of negligence attributed to each of the persons involved. In some cases, the injured person may recover damages only if his or her negligence was no greater than that of the person against whom the suit was filed. Other states have contributory negligence laws which bar an injured person from recovering damages if he or she contributed to the accident.

BASIC COVERAGES

There are six basic types of auto insurance coverage.

Bodily Injury Liability: provides money to pay claims against the policyholder resulting from injuries to pedestrians, persons riding in other cars, or passengers in the policyholder's car. The coverage applies when the car is driven by the policyholder, family members or others who drive the auto with the policyholder's permission. The policyholder and family members also are covered while driving someone else's car with permission.

When claims or lawsuits are brought against the policyholder, bodily injury liability insurance provides protection in the form of legal defense, and if the insurer agrees—or a court decides—that the policyholder is legally liable for the injury, the insurer will pay the damages up to the limits stated in the policy. To protect themselves against the possibility of larger damages, policyholders, usually for a proportionately small extra premium, may elect higher limits than the minimum limits specified in the financial responsibility laws.

GUEST STATUTES

A number of states have "guest statutes" which bar a passenger from taking legal action to recover for injuries unless the driver was guilty of gross negligence.

Medical Payments Insurance: also covers, but without regard to fault, medical expenses resulting from accidental injury related to the automobile. It applies to the policyholder, resident family members and guests in the policyholder's car. It also covers injuries sustained by the policyholder or family members who are injured by a vehicle while walking, or when riding in another car.

Uninsured Motorist Coverage: pays the policyholder and family members for bodily injuries caused by an uninsured motorist or a hit-and-run driver. In most states, it also will pay for injuries caused by a motorist who has auto insurance at the time of the accident but whose insurance company becomes insolvent.

A companion coverage is underinsured motorist insurance, designed to pay the insured's medical expenses in excess of the bodily injury liability limits of another insured driver who is responsible for the injuries. In some states insurers include this feature automatically when higher limits of uninsured motorist coverage are purchased.

Property Damage Liability: pays the costs of claims which result when the policyholder's car damages the property of others. Most often the property is another car, but the coverage includes damage to such property as lamp posts, telephone poles and buildings as well. The policyholder and resident family members also are covered while driving the policyholder's vehicle or, with permission, another car.

If claims or lawsuits are brought against policyholders, property damage liability insurance provides protection in the form of legal defense and payment of damages for which they are determined to be legally liable, up to the limits of the policy.

PHYSICAL DAMAGE COVERAGES

Collision Insurance: pays for damage to the policyholder's car as the result of a collision with another vehicle or other object, or as a result of turning over.

Collision insurance usually is sold with a deductible ranging from $100 to $500.

Even if another driver is at fault, the insurer will pay for its policyholder's repair costs—less the deductible amount. The insurer then may seek reimbursement from the other driver's insurer and, if it is successful, will reimburse its policyholder for the deductible amount.

Comprehensive Insurance: covers losses due to theft, or damage to autos caused by such things as fire, glass breakage, falling objects, missiles, explosion, earthquake, windstorm, hail, flood, vandalism, malicious mischief, or contact with a bird or an animal. Comprehensive physical damage insurance often is sold with a $50 to $250 deductible.

NO-FAULT

In the 1960's, the automobile liability insurance system in effect throughout the U.S. was the target of public criticism. Dissatisfaction was expressed not only by those purchasing auto insurance but by companies and agencies marketing it and by state officials regulating it.

The debate focused on the often expensive and time-consuming process of determining who is at fault—legally liable—when accidents occur. Frequently, this process requires the services of lawyers for both the person suing and the one being sued. Because of the vast number of such cases in some areas, trials and settlements of claims often are subject to long delays. Court decisions and jury awards result in some victims receiving considerably more than their actual losses, some considerably less, and others nothing at all.

These considerations led to the adoption in a number of states of "no-fault" auto insurance laws, under which policyholders recover from their own insurance companies such financial losses as medical and hospital expenses and lost income. In return, policyholders usually are required to relinquish their right to sue except under certain conditions.

LAWSUIT RESTRAINTS

"No-fault" laws vary from state to state. Mainly, features include:

- amount to be paid for medical expenses; or, in case of death, for funeral expenses;
- amount of lost income to be paid to an injured wage earner;
- amount to be paid to a person hired to perform essential services that an injured non-income producer (such as a homemaker) is unable to perform;
- conditions that allow for lawsuits. These usually include death, permanent injury or disfigurement, or a specific amount of medical expenses, referred to as the "threshold for suit," and
- inclusion or exclusion of no-fault payments for property damage.

COST FACTORS

The price, or premium, a car owner pays for auto insurance is conditioned on a number of personal or family considerations, beginning with where the policyholder lives—or, to be precise, where the insured car customarily is kept—and how the car is used.

BASES FOR RATES

Rates on which the premium charges are based are computed separately for each state. Essentially, the rates are built on a foundation of loss experience—the overall frequency and cost of accidents involving insured drivers—together with a trend factor to take into account expected changes in claims costs, such as those resulting from inflation.

Rating Territories

States are divided into rating territories, whose boundaries are determined by such considerations as population density, traffic congestion and other factors which affect exposure to accidents. The premium charged to an individual car owner is affected directly by the number and cost of accidents caused by drivers who live in his or her rating territory.

This latter point bears emphasis. For ratemaking purposes, the cost of an accident is "charged" to the rating territory of the driver who caused it—but not necessarily to the territory in which the accident happened. As an example, if you live in St. Louis and are responsible for an insured accident in Oklahoma City, the cost of the accident will have no effect on Oklahoma City's insurance rates. But it will have an impact on the rates in St. Louis.

RESIDENCE: A KEY ELEMENT

Nevertheless, a community's claim frequency will reflect for the most part accidents that happen locally because a majority of accidents involve local drivers. Records of the National Safety Council show that about three out of four accidents occur within 25 miles of drivers' homes. A community's insurance claim record generally is affected by its own traffic and road conditions, the quality of its traffic law enforcement, and local prices for such things as auto repairs and hospital and medical services.

Driver Classification

Within each community, the cost of auto insurance must be shared by all of its insured drivers. But that cost is not shared equally, because well-documented records make it clear that some groups of drivers have more—and even more costly—accidents than others. For that reason, insurers apply certain factors based on the indicated accident and claim potential of various driver groups.

In most states, age, sex and marital status are recognized as reliable rate-making criteria. The highest rates usually are assigned to youthful drivers who, as a group, have a worse record than older drivers.

AGE OF DRIVER

National Safety Council statistics, developed from state accident reports, show that more than 35 out of every 100 drivers under age 25 are involved in accidents each year. Among drivers in the 25-29 age bracket, about 25 out of 100 have accidents each year. The record for drivers age 30 and up drops to about 16 out of every 100. In other words, drivers in their teens and early 20's are involved in more than twice as many accidents, on the average, as drivers age 30 and older.

Looked at in another way, the data show that persons under 25 represent a little more than 20 per cent of the nation's driving population, but comprise nearly 40 per cent of the drivers involved in accidents.

Among the younger drivers, premiums usually are the highest for unmarried males who own or are the principal operators of cars (young men who drive the family car do less driving than those who have their own cars).

In states in which sex is used as a factor in ratemaking, young women pay lower rates than young men. This is because for many years women have had fewer accidents, on the average, than men (although the gap between the accident rates of the two sexes has been narrowing in recent years).

SEX; MARITAL STATUS

Records indicate that young married people tend to have fewer accidents than young single people. For that reason, usually young married men pay less than young single men for their auto insurance and young married women pay less than young single women.

In some states, all male drivers under age 25 are bracketed in one of two groups (married and unmarried) for ratemaking purposes. More widely used is a system by which rates for unmarried males who drive their own cars are reduced periodically until they reach age 30; for married males and unmarried females, through age 25.

In many states, women in the 30-64 age bracket are allowed premium discounts if they are the only drivers in their households. Also, many drivers over age 65 are eligible for discounts.

Driving Record

Statistics indicate that people who have been responsible for accidents or have been convicted of serious driving violations are more likely to have accidents in the future than are drivers with clear driving records. A system used by many companies calls for premium surcharges for drivers with bad records on the theory that they should more nearly "pay their own way."

PREMIUM SURCHARGES

Usually, the surcharges are imposed on drivers who during the most recent three-year period have had "chargeable" accidents or have been convicted of such serious violations as vehicular homicide, hit-and-run driving or drunk driving. In some cases, surcharges are imposed on the basis of one or more moving traffic violations such as speeding. A chargeable accident generally is one for which the insured is responsible and which results in a death or injury, or property damage in excess of a stipulated dollar amount.

Use of Car

Cars that are driven to and from the job usually are more vulnerable to accidents than cars used only for pleasure purposes. That is because they regularly are exposed to heavy traffic conditions. The same is true of cars used for business purposes throughout the day. Because of this greater exposure to accidents, persons who use their autos in these ways pay higher rates than those who use their cars for pleasure only.

FARMER DISCOUNTS

Conversely, most farmers are allowed premium discounts because their cars seldom are driven under conditions of heavy traffic.

Some companies relate premium charges to the total number of miles a car is driven each year, on the ground that a car whose driver covers, for example, upwards of 20,000 miles a year is more exposed to accident conditions than a car which is driven fewer than 5,000 miles a year.

Type of Car

Low-priced cars cost less to replace, and sometimes less to repair, than higher-priced models. These considerations are taken into account by insurers in establishing premium rates applicable to the collision and comprehensive coverages, which are designed to pay for damages to a policyholder's vehicle.

Some companies use an alternative approach, introduced in the late 1970's, which ties premium costs more closely to the damageability and actual loss experience of automobiles by model year and type.

PREMIUM DISCOUNTS

Many motorists generate their own savings on insurance by driving carefully and thereby avoiding the surcharges imposed as a result of at-fault accidents and serious violations.

In addition, most auto insurance companies offer various kinds of discounts to certain motorists. Eligibility is based on statistical indications that drivers who meet certain conditions are less likely to be involved in accidents. The discounts vary from one company to another and from state to state. Among them:

Driver training discount—for young persons who have completed prescribed driver education courses.

Good student discount—limited to high school or full-time college students age 16 or older. Generally, to qualify, a student must rank among the upper 20 per cent of the class, have a "B" average or better or be on a list indicative of high scholastic achievement.

Resident student discount—offered by some insurers to an insured whose family includes a young driver who is a resident student at a college more than 100 miles from home.

Multi-car discount—usually available to persons who insure two or more cars with the same company.

Air bag discount—available from some companies to drivers of cars equipped with air bags (designed to inflate upon impact for the occupants' protection), which have been shown by studies to save lives and reduce injuries in auto crashes.

Car pool discount—offered by some insurers to members of groups which share each other's cars by forming car pools to get to and from work.

A few companies also offer premium discounts to non-drinkers and non-smokers.

Owners of older cars often drop collision insurance and, in some cases, comprehensive coverages, because of the severely depreciated value of the car. The rationale for taking such a step is that even if the vehicle were to be severely damaged in an accident, the amount the insurer would pay for its repair or replacement would be relatively small (no more than its market value less the amount of the policy's deductible).

AUTOMOBILE INSURANCE PLANS

Some car owners have difficulty in finding, through regular channels, the auto insurance they want and need. Insurers are reluctant to cover those whose poor driving records show them to be bad insurance risks, or who have not been driving long enough to demonstrate a safe driving pattern. Insurers also may be particularly selective during periods of heavy losses.

ASSIGNED RISKS

To accommodate those persons, special facilities have been established in every state and the District of Columbia. Private insurers participate directly in several types of automobile insurance plans (commonly known as "assigned risk plans") in every state except Maryland which has had a state-operated plan (the Maryland Automobile Insurance Fund) since 1973.

Most states operate under a risk assignment system in which an auto insurer's participation is in proportion to the amount of business it writes voluntarily. Each insurer must accept the motorists assigned to it, retaining the profit or absorbing the losses from this "involuntary" class of business.

A few states have adopted alternate plans. These include:

- Reinsurance facilities. Under this system, each auto insurer is required to provide coverage and service the claims for any applicants, but is permitted to transfer a percentage of its poorest risks to the facility. It does so by providing the facility with the names of those risks and keeping it advised of any claims involving them. At the end of the year, each company is reimbursed for any resulting losses, with all companies sharing in those losses through assessments based on their percentage of the total business written voluntarily in the state.

- Joint underwriters' associations (JUAs). In JUA states, several companies which agree to act as "servicing carriers" write and service all of the assigned business. Separate records are kept on this business and auto insurers which do not participate directly as "servicing carriers" share, through assessments, in any losses which are incurred. Those other companies also share in the servicing carriers' costs of handling the business. Each insurance agent in the state is assigned to one of the servicing carriers for the placement of substandard risks.

While private insurers do not participate directly in the Maryland State Fund, they are required by law to subsidize any losses resulting from the Maryland operation, with the cost being charged back against their own policyholders.

SCOPE OF ASSIGNED RISK MARKET

Overall, the various auto insurance plans insure only a relatively small percentage (usually less than 8 per cent) of the insured motorists in the United States. Yet, the shared, or involuntary, market consistently has operated at a financial loss over the years, with the result that the high risk driver is subsidized by car owners who obtain their insurance in the regular marketplace.

THE NONSTANDARD MARKET

Representing still another segment of the automobile insurance marketplace are companies which specialize in hard-to-place "nonstandard" risks whose insurance needs cannot be satisfied either through the standard market or through the various automobile insurance plans.

People with bad accident records or with high-powered or sports cars, for example, may have difficulty obtaining auto insurance through normal channels or may want more coverage than that which is available through many of the assigned risk facilities.

Even the assigned risk plans are not obligated to accept all applicants. Among those who may face rejection are habitual law violators and persons known to engage in illegal enterprises such as gambling operations or dealing in narcotics.

The nonstandard companies offer a market, usually at a higher-than-normal price, for such persons, as well as for others who are acceptable to the assigned risk plans but who want more than the limited amount of coverage some of those plans offer.

UNSATISFIED JUDGMENT FUNDS

DEFAULTED AWARDS

A few states have established unsatisfied court judgment funds to pay auto accident victims at least a portion of any judgment against a negligent motorist when all other efforts to collect payment have failed. In some cases, the funds also pay the costs of injuries sustained in hit-and-run accidents. Compensation is not available, however, to anyone who is an uninsured car owner.

Each fund has a cap on the amount of money it will pay to an accident victim. The funds are financed either through assessments against automobile insurance companies operating in the state or by funds collected from motor vehicle registration fees.

Once a fund has paid an unsatisfied judgment, the legally liable motorist is deprived of his or her driving privileges until restitution to the fund, plus interest, has been made.

Some states have assigned claims plans which compensate accident victims for uncollectible judgments. In those states, individual insurers are assigned, on a rotating basis, to investigate and settle the claims. The companies are reimbursed from a fund to which all insurers doing business in the state contribute.

MOTORCYCLE INSURANCE

INSURANCE FOR MOPEDS

Although motorcycles are not classified as automobiles for insurance purposes, insurance for motorcycles—as well as for mopeds, snowmobiles and other "miscellaneous vehicles"—is quite similar to auto insurance. In fact, auto policies—with endorsements—are used to provide coverage for such vehicles. Most of the states which require car owners to have liability insurance extend that requirement to motorcyclists as well.

A car owner who also has a motorcycle may insure the bike through an endorsement to the auto policy. The coverages available to motorcyclists are bodily injury and property damage liability, medical payments (usually limited to $500), uninsured motorist coverage and physical damage coverage including collision. Some insurance companies offer six-month or nine-month policies to persons who live in colder climates and retire their motorcycles during the winter months.

HOME INSURANCE

For many people who buy their homes, the purchase cost may be the largest single investment they'll make. For most home owners and renters, the regular mortgage or rent payment amounts to a significant percentage of their income.

To protect their investment, many people install fire extinguishers, smoke detectors, burglar alarms, locks and other devices. Most also purchase insurance as a safeguard against unforeseen financial losses resulting from damage to or destruction of property.

Insurance coverages for the home, its contents, and the home owner's or tenant's liability to others usually are combined into a single package (homeowners) policy, although separate policies are available for fire, theft and other perils. The principal features of the various forms of the homeowners policy are described below.

HOMEOWNERS PROPERTY COVERAGES

POLICY CHOICES

Those who own or rent their homes may choose from among several versions of the homeowners package policy which differ primarily as to the number of perils that the insurer agrees to cover.

Homeowners Policies HO-1, HO-2, HO-5

As the chart on page 24 indicates, the basic homeowners policy (HO-1) provides coverage against 11 specified perils, the broad form (HO-2) covers the same 11 perils and seven others, and the comprehensive form (HO-5) covers all perils except a few which are specifically excluded.

Homeowners policies cover not only the dwelling, but other structures on the same property such as a garage or a tool shed. Personal belongings—furniture, appliances, clothing and other possessions—also are covered, although coverage of certain valuables such as furs, jewelry, antiques and collections is strictly limited. Policies may be written to cover the property of guests while they are on the policyholder's premises. Automobiles and pets are not covered, however.

ADDITIONAL LIVING EXPENSES

Another feature of the homeowners policy is that it will pay any additional living expenses (over and above normal expenditures) made necessary should the policyholder and family need to live elsewhere temporarily because of damage to the home caused by an insured peril. This feature also applies in the event of an evacuation ordered by a civil authority because of damage to nearby areas by a peril listed in the policy.

If the home owner rents a portion of the insured dwelling, he or she will be reimbursed for the fair rental value if the rent income is lost because the house is not habitable.

A Special Policy (HO-3)

Many home owners want the broadest insurance coverage available for their dwelling and other structures on the premises, but do not want to pay for this same extensive coverage on their personal property. Their needs are met by a special form (HO-3), which provides the same "all-risk" coverage for their dwelling and other structures on the property as does the comprehensive form (HO-5), while limiting coverage of their personal property to the 18 perils included in the broad form (HO-2).

Renter's Policy (HO-4)

The tenants policy, or contents broad form (HO-4), is designed for those who rent an apartment or house or own a cooperative apartment. It insures household contents and personal belongings against all of the perils included in the broad form (HO-2). Coverage for the building or buildings is the responsibility of the landlord or cooperative association. The renter's policy does provide coverage for additional living expenses, however.

Condominium Unit-Owner's Policy (HO-6)

A condominium association usually buys the insurance to cover the condominium's property (buildings and structures) and liability. However, a special condominium unit-owner's policy (HO-6) is available for unit owners who wish to insure their personal property or to cover any additions or alterations which are not insured by the association's policy. Coverages are basically the same as provided by the renter's policy (HO-4).

PERILS AGAINST WHICH PROPERTIES ARE INSURED UNDER THE VARIOUS HOMEOWNERS POLICIES

BASIC HO-1	BROAD HO-2	SPECIAL HO-3	RENTER'S HO-4	COMPRE-HENSIVE HO-5	CONDO-MINIUM HO-6	OLDER HOME HO-8	PERILS
Dwelling and Personal Property	Dwelling and Personal Property	Dwelling only; Personal Property only	Personal Property only	Dwelling and Personal Property	Personal Property only	Dwelling and Personal Property	1. Fire or lightning
Dwelling and Personal Property	Dwelling and Personal Property	Dwelling only; Personal Property only	Personal Property only	Dwelling and Personal Property	Personal Property only	Dwelling and Personal Property	2. Loss of property removed from premises endangered by fire or other perils*
Dwelling and Personal Property	Dwelling and Personal Property	Dwelling only; Personal Property only	Personal Property only	Dwelling and Personal Property	Personal Property only	Dwelling and Personal Property	3. Windstorm or hail
Dwelling and Personal Property	Dwelling and Personal Property	Dwelling only; Personal Property only	Personal Property only	Dwelling and Personal Property	Personal Property only	Dwelling and Personal Property	4. Explosion
Dwelling and Personal Property	Dwelling and Personal Property	Dwelling only; Personal Property only	Personal Property only	Dwelling and Personal Property	Personal Property only	Dwelling and Personal Property	5. Riot or civil commotion
Dwelling and Personal Property	Dwelling and Personal Property	Dwelling only; Personal Property only	Personal Property only	Dwelling and Personal Property	Personal Property only	Dwelling and Personal Property	6. Aircraft
Dwelling and Personal Property	Dwelling and Personal Property	Dwelling only; Personal Property only	Personal Property only	Dwelling and Personal Property	Personal Property only	Dwelling and Personal Property	7. Vehicles
Dwelling and Personal Property	Dwelling and Personal Property	Dwelling only; Personal Property only	Personal Property only	Dwelling and Personal Property	Personal Property only	Dwelling and Personal Property	8. Smoke
Dwelling and Personal Property	Dwelling and Personal Property	Dwelling only; Personal Property only	Personal Property only	Dwelling and Personal Property	Personal Property only	Dwelling and Personal Property	9. Vandalism and malicious mischief
Dwelling and Personal Property	Dwelling and Personal Property	Dwelling only; Personal Property only	Personal Property only	Dwelling and Personal Property	Personal Property only	Dwelling and Personal Property	10. Theft
Dwelling and Personal Property	Dwelling and Personal Property	Dwelling only; Personal Property only	Personal Property only	Dwelling and Personal Property	Personal Property only	Dwelling and Personal Property	11. Breakage of glass constituting a part of the building
	Dwelling and Personal Property	Dwelling only; Personal Property only	Personal Property only	Dwelling and Personal Property	Personal Property only		12. Falling objects
	Dwelling and Personal Property	Dwelling only; Personal Property only	Personal Property only	Dwelling and Personal Property	Personal Property only		13. Weight of ice, snow, sleet
	Dwelling and Personal Property	Dwelling only; Personal Property only	Personal Property only	Dwelling and Personal Property	Personal Property only		14. Collapse of building(s) or any part thereof
	Dwelling and Personal Property	Dwelling only; Personal Property only	Personal Property only	Dwelling and Personal Property	Personal Property only		15. Sudden and accidental tearing asunder, cracking, burning, or bulging of a steam or hot water heating system or of appliances for heating water
	Dwelling and Personal Property	Dwelling only; Personal Property only	Personal Property only	Dwelling and Personal Property	Personal Property only		16. Accidental discharge, leakage or overflow of water or steam from within a plumbing, heating or air-conditioning system or domestic appliance
	Dwelling and Personal Property	Dwelling only; Personal Property only	Personal Property only	Dwelling and Personal Property	Personal Property only		17. Freezing of plumbing, heating and air-conditioning systems and domestic appliances
	Dwelling and Personal Property	Dwelling only; Personal Property only	Personal Property only	Dwelling and Personal Property	Personal Property only		18. Sudden and accidental injury from artificially generated currents to electrical appliances, devices, fixtures and wiring (TV and radio tubes not included)
		Dwelling only		Dwelling and Personal Property			All perils except flood, earthquake, war, nuclear accident and others specified in your policy. Check your policy for a complete listing of perils excluded.

— Dwelling and Personal Property
— Dwelling only
— Personal Property only

*Included as a peril in traditional forms of the homeowners policy; as an additional coverage in the simplified (HO-76) policies.

Older Home Insurance (HO-8)

Most homeowners policies provide for damage to a building to be paid for on the basis of replacement costs without deduction for depreciation if the policyholder carries insurance for at least 80 per cent of the replacement costs.

Older homes, however, usually are so constructed that it is not economically feasible to duplicate them following a loss. Ornate woodwork or Victorian design, for example, might be so expensive to restore in its original form that neither the property owner nor the insurer would be willing to incur the costs involved.

MARKET VALUE COVERAGE

The HO-8 policy is designed to aid these home owners by allowing them to carry lower limits of insurance—such as the market value of the home—rather than the 80 per cent of replacement cost used for newer houses. In effect, the policy contemplates returning the property to serviceable condition, but not necessarily with the use of materials of the same kind and quality as the original.

This policy insures the property against the same perils as the basic form (HO-1), but restricts coverage of losses by theft to a maximum of $1,000.

Mobilehome Owner's Policy

There is also a special policy for persons who own and occupy a mobilehome that is at least 10 by 40 feet long. The mobilehome policy provides basically the same coverages as the homeowners broad form policy (HO-2). Because of the difference in construction and the greater susceptibility of mobile homes to wind damage, premiums for these policies are substantially higher than for a similar policy on a conventional house.

SIMPLIFIED HOMEOWNERS POLICIES—THE HO-76 PROGRAM

PLAIN TALK POLICIES

To help make policies more readily understandable to members of the public, the insurance business in recent years has been developing policies which substitute easy-to-read wording for the more legal language which traditionally has been used.

The homeowners 76 program, so-named because of its introduction in 1976, is a series of simplified versions of policies HO-1 through HO-6. Generally, the simplified policies are briefer—some of them containing 5,000 fewer words—but still contain the equivalent information.

An example of the wording changes in the same section of the new and traditional homeowners policies:

New	Traditional
"We will provide the insurance described in this policy in return for the premium and compliance with all applicable provisions of this policy."	"In Consideration of the Provisions and Stipulations Herein or Added Hereto and of the Premium Above Specified, this Company, for the term shown above at noon, (Standard Time) to expiration date shown above at noon (Standard Time) at location of property involved, to an amount . . ."

The revisions of these policies included some minor changes in the coverages, primarily to recognize today's inflated values. These changes have not altered rating or price structures, however. For example, coverage of trees, shrubs, plants or lawns is increased from $250 to $500 in the HO-76 policies and credit card, forgery and counterfeit money coverage of $500—offered as an option in the traditional policies—is automatically included. Rowboats and canoes, on thc other hand, were covered against windstorm while anywhere on the insured premises in the traditional policies, but are covered only while in a fully enclosed building (like any other watercraft) in the HO-76 version.

REVISIONS IN COVERAGE

ADDITIONAL COVERAGES

When a fire or other peril damages or destroys á house, there are expenses that go beyond the repair of the house itself. Insurers have added six of these "after-the-fact" expenses to the coverages for persons who own houses and have homeowners policies. The sixth additional coverage applies also to renter's, condominium and mobilehome policies.

- Debris removal. Insurers will pay the reasonable expense of taking damaged property away.
- Reasonable repairs. Where temporary repairs are necessary to protect property from further damage, insurers will pay for the additional expense.
- Trees, shrubs, and other plants. Insurers will pay for certain insured perils (not including windstorm) up to $500 for any tree, shrub or plant or an overall maximum of 5

per cent of the limit of insurance for the dwelling. Lawns also are covered.

- Fire department service charge. In areas where property owners must pay for fire department services, insurers will reimburse policyholders up to $250.
- Property removal. When property is rescued from a dwelling, this coverage protects it for up to 30 days against direct loss from any cause.
- Credit card, forgery, and counterfeit money. Insurers will reimburse policyholders up to $500 should they lose their credit cards and others charge purchases to their accounts. The same limit applies to check forgery or a policyholder's loss resulting from acceptance in good faith of counterfeit money.

PERSONAL ARTICLES COVERAGE

Certain property in the home may be more valuable than the limits set under the personal property coverage of a homeowners or tenants policy—items such as antique furniture, furs, camera equipment, coin and stamp collections, jewelry, art pieces and other expensive or unusual properties.

These valuables may be insured by purchasing a personal articles "floater" as a separate coverage or by endorsement to the homeowners policy. The term, "floater," derives from the fact that the coverage applies wherever the property is located at the time of loss. The coverage, in effect, "floats" with the property.

SAFE DEPOSIT BOXES

Because the homeowners policy provides only limited coverage of items which many people keep in safe deposit boxes, some companies offer a separate safe deposit box insurance policy to supplement that protection. Generally, such policies provide all-risk coverage for securities and burglary and robbery coverage for other valuables.

FLOOD AND EARTHQUAKE INSURANCE

Homeowners policies do not cover damage resulting from floods or earthquake. However, persons who live in flood or earthquake prone areas can purchase separate property insurance coverages, subject to deductibles, against these perils.

The Federal Insurance Administration offers a program to make flood insurance available in many areas. The fact that flood insurance is marketable only to people who live in areas likely to be flooded makes it generally uneconomical for private insurers to provide this coverage. To qualify for flood coverage, property must be located in a community that has agreed to implement land-use control measures to reduce losses from future flooding. Thousands of communities participate in the program. Property owners can find out if the coverage is available in their community by contacting any insurance agent or broker.

Since earthquakes strike most often in the Pacific Coast area, more than half of all earthquake policies are purchased in California. Nevertheless, most states are vulnerable to earthquakes and insurance coverage is available through private insurers. Earthquake insurance usually is written as an addition to a fire, homeowners or other property insurance policy.

INSURANCE AGAINST VOLCANIC ERUPTIONS

Damage from volcanos as a risk to be insured against did not readily come to most persons' minds—until May 18, 1980, when Washington State's Mount St. Helens began a series of calamitous activities that resulted in millions of dollars in property damage.

IMPACT OF MOUNT ST. HELENS

The volcanic activity at Mount St. Helens created confusion about insurance coverage. Traditional homeowners policies specifically excluded "volcanic eruptions," but the simplified homeowners policies (HO-76 series) did not have this exclusion. Each type of policy, however, covers "explosions," and insurers relied on that coverage in paying the vast majority of policyholders' property damage claims in the blast area.

The months after the initial eruption saw the industry and regulators conferring on how to avoid confusion should such an event face them again. At year end 1980, the Washington insurance commissioner issued a bulletin which began:

> While the insurance industry responded well to losses resulting from the unprecedented eruptions of Mount St. Helens, it became evident that greater clarity was needed in the language of homeowners and dwelling fire insurance policies with respect to volcano coverage. Accordingly, representatives of a cross-section of insurers have assisted my office in the development of a suitable endorsement.

The bulletin promulgated a rule, to be effective July 1, 1981, requiring homeowners and dwelling fire insurance policies "that provide coverage for damage resulting from volcanic eruptions" to spell out precisely how the coverage applies.

LIABILITY COVERAGES

All forms of the homeowners policy include liability coverages which apply not only to the policyholder but to all family members who reside in the home. These coverages include liability, medical payments to others and physical damage to the property of others.

Personal Liability

The liability coverage is designed to provide protection against a claim or a lawsuit which could cripple a home owner financially. Suppose, for example, that a visitor slips and falls on a policyholder's property, suffers a head injury which results in impaired vision, and eventually sues for $100,000 or more. Or, suppose that as a result of a policyholder's misjudgment in felling a tree in the back yard, the house next door is damaged extensively and the owner files a claim. If it is agreed by the parties involved, or decided by a court, that the policyholder is legally liable for the visitor's injury or the damage to the neighbor's property, the insurance company will pay the damages assessed up to the limits of the policy. Further, in case of a lawsuit, the insurance company will pay the legal costs of defense whether or not the policyholder ultimately is held to be legally responsible.

DEFENSE COSTS COVERED

The minimum liability limit for each form of the homeowners policy is $25,000, but larger amounts can be purchased. The two examples just mentioned deal with accidents occurring on or near the home owner's property. However, accidents occurring elsewhere (not including business-related accidents) are covered in the same way if they are caused by the policyholder, a family member or a pet.

Medical Payments

Often, accidents result in minor injuries which are inexpensive to treat but which could become relatively burdensome in terms of both time and dollars if payment of the bills were dependent on establishing legal liability. The medical payments section of every homeowners policy provides for payment of such bills without regard to fault in case of injuries to others on the policyholder's premises. It also applies elsewhere to injuries caused by the policyholder, a family member or a pet. The basic amount of protection is $500 for each person injured, but larger amounts may be purchased.

THE FAMILY PET

While this coverage does not pay for injuries to the policyholder or family members, it does enable the policyholder to discharge what he or she may believe to be a moral obligation to pay for someone else's medical expenses under certain conditions.

The personal liability and medical payments coverages apply even to boats under certain conditions—and to golf carts when they are being used for golfing purposes. The home owner's liability is covered if the boat he or she owns or rents is an inboard or inboard-outboard powered boat of 50 horsepower or less, or a sailboat less than 26 feet long. Also, liability arising from the ownership of an outboard powered boat with not more than 25 horsepower is covered.

GOLF CARTS, BOATS

Supplementary Coverage

An important supplementary coverage in all homeowners policies pays for minor damage that you or someone in your family might cause accidentally to another person's property, regardless of who is at fault or, as is sometimes the case, when no one is at fault. Damage caused intentionally by children under age 13 is covered because it is considered to be accidental. However, the maximum amount that an insurance company will agree to pay under supplementary coverage for any one incident is $250.

Workers' Compensation

Although workers' compensation insurance generally is thought of as a coverage for business and industry (see page 64), it also is available to homeowners and renters to cover domestic employees—either part-time or full-time.

Two states, New Hampshire and New Jersey, now require that every policy issued to private individuals which affords comprehensive personal liability coverage—such as the homeowners and renter's policies—include workers' compensation coverage for household employees. In California, any home owner who employs domestic workers on either a full-time or part-time basis is required to have workers' compensation coverage.

PARTIAL LOSSES

HOW MUCH COVERAGE?

In order to receive full replacement payment for any partial loss or damage under a homeowners policy (with the exception of the special policies for older homes), the owner must insure the dwelling for at least 80 per cent of its replacement value. For a home with a replacement value of $80,000, as an example, coverage in the amount of $64,000 (80 per cent) meets the requirements of this provision. If a fire should result in $5,000 damage to the living room, the insurer would pay that amount, less the amount of the deductible, to cover the necessary repairs.

Should the same house be insured for less than $64,000, any payment for a partial loss would be reduced. The reduction is calculated in one of two possible ways. Assuming coverage of $40,000 (instead of the $64,000 of coverage the owner should have), the owner would stand to collect either forty sixty-fourths of the $5,000 loss ($3,125), or the actual cash value (replacement cost less depreciation), whichever is larger. Of course, in the event of a total loss, the insurer would pay no more than the amount of coverage ($40,000 in this example).

BASIS OF COVERAGE

Insurers stress that the market value of a house is not a proper basis for determining the amount of coverage to buy. Home owners should consult with their agent or broker for assistance in determining replacement value.

With policies covering homes, the amount of coverage on the house becomes the basis for determining amounts of coverage which are automatically assigned to other structures on the property, personal property and additional living expenses. The other structures are covered for 10 per cent of the amount of coverage on the house; personal property, for 50 per cent, and additional living expenses, for 20 per cent (10 per cent under the basic policy, HO-1). For a detailed breakdown of the coverages, see table, page 32.

Renter's policies provide a minimum of $4,000 coverage on personal property, 10 per cent of that amount to cover additions and alterations to the dwelling unit and 20 per cent of the amount of personal property coverage for additional living expenses. Condominium policies cover personal property for a minimum of $4,000, and 40 per cent of the amount of that coverage for additional living expenses and $1,000 for additions and alterations to the unit.

The table on page 32 summarizes the amounts of the principal coverages, under a homeowners policy, on an $80,000 house insured to the full amount of its replacement cost and insured to 80 per cent of its replacement value.

HOUSEHOLD INVENTORIES

Insurers strongly recommend that policyholders make an inventory of all household furnishings and personal belongings for their own protection in deciding how much insurance to buy, and for use in the event of a loss. The inventory, along with photographs of important items and receipts covering major purchases, should be stored in a safe place away from home.

AMOUNTS OF COVERAGES UNDER THE BROAD FORM HOMEOWNERS POLICY (HO-2)*

(Assuming a house with an $80,000 replacement value insured to full value and to 80% of value)

Property Coverages	Insured to Replacement Value		Insured to 80% of Replacement Value	
Dwelling	$80,000	(full value)	$64,000	(80% of full value)
Other Structures on Property	8,000	(10% of dwelling)	6,400	(10% of dwelling)
Unscheduled Personal Property	40,000	(50% of dwelling)**	32,000	(50% of dwelling)**
Additional Living Expenses	16,000	(20% of dwelling)	12,800	(20% of dwelling)
Trees, Shrubs and Plants	4,000	(5% of dwelling, subject to maximum of $500 per item)	3,200	(5% of dwelling, subject to maximum of $500 per item)
Liability Coverages				
Personal Liability	$25,000	(each occurrence)**	$25,000	(each occurrence)**
Medical payments to Others (regardless of fault)	500	(each person)**	500	(each person)**
Damage to Property of Others (regardless of fault)	250	(each occurrence)	250	(each occurrence)

* Amounts of coverages are the same under the basic form (HO-1), the special form (HO-3) and the comprehensive form (HO-5) except that additional living expenses under the basic form are covered only up to 10% of the amount of coverage on the dwelling.

** Larger amounts are available.

KEEPING PACE WITH INFLATION

Insurance to Value

Pointing to the sharp increase in home values during the 1970's and into the 1980's, insurers emphasize the importance to home owners of reviewing regularly—at least once a year—the amount of insurance coverage on their property.

Studies have shown that many thousands of home owners are underinsured because they haven't kept pace with inflation by increasing the amount of their coverage, although most companies and their representatives regularly recommend higher policy limits—if warranted—when policies are due for renewal. Some companies automatically increase coverage each year, in line with inflation, unless the policyholder objects.

Widely available to home owners is an inflation guard endorsement which periodically increases the amount of coverage under a homeowners policy as protection against the effect of inflation. Typical of such an endorsement is one which provides for an automatic increase every three months in the amount of protection afforded by the policy, at the rate of 1 per cent of the original amount of coverage.

PROPERTY INSURANCE PLANS

The insurance industry operates special property insurance plans in many states to assure the availability of insurance protection for high-risk properties or for properties in coastal areas vulnerable to severe windstorm damage, where insurance otherwise might be difficult to obtain.

FAIR PLANS

About half of the states have property insurance plans known as FAIR Plans, an acronym for Fair Access to Insurance Requirements. The plans as they operate today were established following passage by Congress of the Housing and Urban Development Act of 1968, which provided for federal riot reinsurance to those states which instituted such property insurance pools. In 1980, there were FAIR Plans in 26 states, the District of Columbia and Puerto Rico.

The FAIR Plans are supported by the insurers that write insurance voluntarily on other properties in the state. Any plan, in order to qualify for riot reinsurance under current federal law, must offer insurance on inner-city properties at rates no higher than those of the voluntary market, with the result that many of the plans consistently have sustained operating losses. New York and a few other states have elected to set rates at a level designed to make the plans more nearly self-sustaining, rather than to continue federal riot reinsurance.

Following the riots in the mid and late 1960's, arson has developed as a more serious problem than riot in the inner-city areas. Along with numerous other loss prevention activities, the insurance industry has supported vigorous anti-arson programs nationwide.

All of the FAIR plans offer fire and extended coverage (windstorm, vandalism, and certain additional coverages) on residences and commercial properties. A number of the plans now offer homeowners, commercial package policies and some miscellaneous coverages as well.

BEACH PLANS

Counterparts to the FAIR plans are beach and windstorm insurance plans operated by property insurers in seven states along the Atlantic and Gulf Coasts to assure availability of insurance for both residences and commercial properties against damage from hurricanes or other windstorms.

FARM INSURANCE

The traditional family-owned farm or ranch has special insurance needs. Some property, such as the farmhouse and personal belongings, can be covered like the property of any other home owner. But much or all of the property necessary to the farmer's business operation—barns, sheds, farm equipment and machinery, hay, grain and more—is not covered by the standard homeowners policy.

Making matters more complicated are the liability questions that could arise because of the overlapping uses of the property. If another person trips over a tractor attachment stored near the farm home and an injury claim results, who is responsible, the farmer or the farmer's business?

To best accommodate this market, insurers have developed a farmowners-ranchowners policy which combines personal and business coverages in a single package policy.

MULTI-PURPOSE PACKAGE

The policy is similar in design and content to the one used for home owners except that it is in several parts—one for the farmhouse and personal property, and others to protect the farmer against certain perils and liabilities which can cause losses to the farmer's business assets.

(Large, corporate farms often mix and match various coverages to suit their individual needs. Insurance companies often create package policies tailored specifically for these agribusinesses.)

DWELLING AND PERSONAL PROPERTY COVERAGES

Under the farmowners-ranchowners policy, three types of coverage for the farmer's home and nonbusiness property are available: basic, broad and tenant's coverages. There is no farmowners package policy comparable to the comprehensive, ''all-risk'' coverage offered to other home owners.

Insurers suggest—but do not require—that farmers inventory

all properties and their respective values for use in case of a loss.

In order for the farmer to collect either the full replacement cost or the full repair cost (whichever is less) of damaged or lost property, the property must be insured to at least 80 per cent of its replacement cost.

Basic Coverage (FR-1)

This covers the farmer's house and all personal property as well as additional living expenses or loss of rental income should the home be rendered uninhabitable because of damage caused by an insured peril. The perils covered by this policy are fire, theft, windstorm or hail, explosion, riot or civil commotion, aircraft, vehicles, smoke, vandalism and malicious mischief, and damage to personal property resulting from the overturn of a vehicle. The policy covers loss of property removed from the farm because it is endangered by an insured peril.

Although similar to the basic homeowners policy, there are significant differences. Aside from the dwelling, the only structures on the premises which are covered are private garages (for 10 percent of the dollar limit set for the house). Lawns, trees and shrubs are not covered, nor is glass breakage.

Broad Coverage (FR-2)

This policy insures the farmhouse and nonbusiness personal property against the same perils listed in the broad form of the homeowners policy. (See page 24.)

Tenants Broad Coverage (FR-4)

Some farms and farmhouses are rented. This coverage provides the tenant with insurance protection against the same perils as the FR-2 policy, but only for the personal property kept at the location—property not used for business purposes. No coverage is provided for the dwelling, since any losses would be borne by the owner.

FARM EQUIPMENT AND LIVESTOCK

In most areas, farmers using the package policy have two options for covering their "farm personal" property, including equipment and livestock but excluding farm buildings. One option, which is available in all states, permits the farmer to itemize—or schedule—such property. The second choice, available in some areas, is a blanket form of coverage.

Both insure against the perils of fire and lightning, removal of debris, windstorm, hail, explosion, riot or civil commotion, aircraft or vehicle collision, smoke, theft, vandalism and malicious mischief, and electrocution of livestock.

Scheduled Farm Personal Property (FR-6)

The property the farmer may list under this coverage is that which is usual to the operation of a farm—including hay, grain, fertilizers, machinery, farm vehicles and equipment, farm records and even livestock. In some cases, the coverage may be extended to stored goods such as tobacco, vegetables and fruit which are not insured under the blanket coverage.

Blanket Coverage (Unscheduled Farm Property)(FR-7)

This coverage "blankets," for insurance purposes, most farm personal property on the farmer's premises. Most, but not all. For example, while the blanket coverage applies to goats, horses, mules and donkeys—other animals and poultry are not included. Also, certain crop yields such as tobacco, cotton, vegetables and fruit are not covered.

The blanket coverage generally is more expensive than the scheduled property option, and is not available everywhere.

FARM BUILDINGS

Barns and other farm structures, including dwellings other than the main farmhouse, are covered under the FR-8 section of the farmowners package policy.

The structure, including portable sheds, are insured against losses caused by fire, lightning, windstorm or hail, explosion, smoke, riot or civil commotion, damage by aircraft or vehicle, vandalism and malicious mischief. The cost of debris removal also is covered.

LIABILITY

BROADER THAN HOMEOWNERS

The liability coverage provided in the farmowners-ranchowners package, FR-9, is similar to that offered under the homeowners policy (see page 29), except that it also applies to the liability resulting from the farmer's business operations. Thus, it would cover a claim by a person who was injured on the farm whether it be in the farmhouse, in the cattle barn, or in the open.

Liabilities arising from the operation of a roadside stand to sell the farmer's own produce are also covered, and product liability coverage is included as long as the products are of a farm nature.

Some farmers do what insurers call custom farming—incidental farm-related work for others. The policy covers their liability while engaged in such operations, although an extra premium may be required if custom farming is done frequently.

Finally, domestic employees or household workers whose duties do not relate to the farmer's business are covered for medical payments in the event of a bodily injury sustained while on the farmer's land. In some states, this section of the policy may be extended to include farm workers as well.

OPTIONAL COVERAGES

There are two options the farmer or ranchowner can add to the package for an extra premium. The medical payments coverage of the liability section can be expanded to include family members who might be injured while working on the farm.

ANIMAL COLLISION

The other option, an interesting one, is called animal collision. If a cow, horse, hog, sheep or goat is hit by another person's vehicle on a public highway, insurers will reimburse the farmer up to $400 per animal.

"ALL-RISK" ENDORSEMENTS

Some farmers desire greater coverage than the FR policy alone provides. Insurers have made available supplementary coverages which may be added to the basic FR package by endorsement. Two of the most popular are all-risk coverage for mobile agricultural equipment and for livestock.

These all-risk endorsements require that the farmer list all the property to be covered on the policy. The property is then insured against every peril except those specifically excluded in the policy. The livestock endorsement excludes loss by mysterious disappearance, escape or accidental shooting by the farmer or farm help, while the equipment endorsement excludes damage from wear and tear, severe temperature changes, mechanical or electrical breakdown, or damage resulting from lack of maintenance.

FARM AUTO INSURANCE DISCOUNT

Persons engaged in farming or ranching may qualify for a discount on their auto insurance premiums for a private passenger car, a station wagon, a motor vehicle with a pick-up body, a delivery sedan or a panel truck.

To qualify for the farmer discount, a "farm automobile" must not be used in any occupation other than farming or ranching, nor used in driving to and from an occupation other than farming.

CROP-HAIL INSURANCE

A day may come when weather patterns can be controlled or modified. Until such a time, however, insurance offers the primary means of protection against potential financial ruin because of damage to crops by the elements.

The first crop policy was issued more than a century ago with hail as its basic peril. Currently, it is available in all states and is sold by private insurance companies with competition from the Federal Crop Insurance Corporation, an agency of the U.S. Department of Agriculture.

A variety of crop-hail policies is available, each with its own set of coverages and exclusions. While the Crop-Hail Insurance Association has produced a simplified standard policy, coverages generally differ from one state to another. Coverages are tailored to take into account differences in climates and other environmental factors.

Crop-hail policies share common characteristics. In nearly every case, the coverage becomes effective once the crop is above the ground, and expires when the crop is harvested. Also, the limits of coverage are expressed in terms of acreage rather than the total value of the crop.

Until 1980, private insurers insured only against the perils of fire, lightning, hail and wind (if accompanied by hail which destroys at least 5 per cent of the crop). The federal government, however, offered "all-risk" policies on a limited geographical basis. The all-risk policy, in effect, covers crops against such additional perils as insects, excessive moisture, drought and any other peril not specifically excluded.

ALL-RISK INNOVATION

Private insurers were hesitant to offer such extensive coverage due to the greater-than-average degree of risk involved. The passage of the Federal Crop Insurance Act of 1980, however, made it feasible for private insurers to offer "all-risk" policies because they can reinsure them with the federal government. The Act also requires the Federal Crop Insurance Corporation to use private insurance agents wherever possible to place federal policies and gives the agents the right to renew and service the policies. Under the program, farmers countrywide have access to the full crop insurance coverage they need.

COMMERCIAL LINES

COMMERCIAL INSURANCE

More than half of all property/casualty insurance written is commercial insurance—that is, insurance on businesses, organizations and institutions, and their properties.

Coverages are available for nearly all mobile and stationary business properties against a variety of perils. Liability insurance also is available for a wide range of exposures, providing for the defense of lawsuits against the business, as well as payments for any claims, awards or other settlements to workers or members of the public.

In addition, insurers offer protection against losses due to interruption of business, employee dishonesty, failure in performance of another person or firm, and other risks.

The financial losses that a business or organization may be exposed to during its daily operation can originate from almost any aspect of the business. Along with safety and security, insurance protection can assure owners of businesses that these losses will be minimized or made less debilitating than if the companies assumed the risks themselves.

INSURANCE SURVEY

While the need for coverage against fire, windstorm, explosion, liability hazards and other perils generally is obvious, only a careful analysis will disclose the amount and the types of insurance that will meet the needs of a specific commercial enterprise. The value of business property and the nature of the various exposures must be considered in determining precisely what kinds of insurance are needed. An insurance survey, a service provided by agents, brokers or individual companies, is available for this purpose.

Once the exposures are determined, a business has the option of purchasing coverages separately or choosing from a variety of package policies designed to cover most ordinary business risks.

While many single coverages and package policies are standardized, insurers offer a large number of options which allow flexibility for tailoring of coverages to fit the needs of individual policyholders. Such options are in the form of endorsements, variations in limits and deductibles and new combinations of coverage which may be offered by individual companies.

WIDE RANGE OF SERVICES

In today's competitive insurance market, more and more companies are providing not only insurance, but a wide range of other services. These services include loss control measures such as equipment inspections, hazard surveys, safety program coordination and injured worker rehabilitation programs. In addition, insurers offer loss adjusting, loss data processing and analysis, analyses of present insurance coverages, recommendations for risk-associated cash management, planning for future insurance needs and other risk management functions.

COMMERCIAL AUTO INSURANCE

Many of the principles which apply to personal automobile insurance coverages also apply to commercial vehicles. (See Auto Insurance—page 12.) Businesses, like individuals, are concerned with protecting the investments they have in vehicles and they also must be concerned about the legal liability associated with the operation of these vehicles. Most businesses use insurance programs to cover the loss of or damage to their equipment and to cover their liability exposures.

THREE CLASSES

There are three main classifications of business automobiles for insurance purposes. These are: (1) private passenger automobiles owned by businesses, (2) trucks and (3) public conveyance vehicles, which include any type of vehicle used to carry passengers. Privately owned automobiles which are used for business purposes are insured under personal automobile insurance policies but usually at a higher rate—reflecting the increased use of the vehicles—than would be charged for non-business uses.

Businesses also frequently buy insurance covering their liability for their employees' use of automobiles not owned by the business, including personally owned cars as well as rented, leased or borrowed vehicles.

Business automobile insurance can be written on a fleet basis, in which case all or a specified category of automobiles owned by a business are included in one policy. Usually, fleet policies are written so that newly-acquired vehicles are automatically covered. Businesses with a limited number of vehicles usually insure the vehicles individually.

PRICING FACTORS

The price of commercial automobile insurance depends principally on five factors. These are (1) the use of the vehicles, including the types of cargoes, (2) the number of vehicles (discounts usually are applied to fleets of five or more vehicles), (3) the size of the vehicles, (4) the territory in which the vehicles are principally garaged, (5) the radius of operations. In many cases, rules governing the type and the amount of insurance have been established by regulatory authorities. For example, the Interstate Commerce Commission sets minimum limits for liability insurance for all common carriers and contract carriers operating in interstate or foreign commerce. In addition, many states require liability limits higher than those set by the ICC, particularly for haulers who carry dangerous cargoes.

An important type of business automobile insurance covers vehicles used to carry passengers for a charge—including taxicabs, school buses, airport buses, chartered buses, sightseeing buses and general passenger service buses. In many cases, federal and state agencies specify minimum amounts of liability insurance required for these vehicles.

As in other areas, the insurance industry has created a number of special coverages to meet certain business owners' insurance needs for motor vehicles. These include such policies as garage keeper's liability and automobile dealers physical damage insurance.

AVIATION INSURANCE

Like commercial auto insurance, the commercial aircraft policy includes both physical damage and liability coverages. There are, however, marked differences in the nature of aircraft exposures compared to those of autos. Aircraft insurance is considered to be a specialty line not only because there are fewer aircraft than autos, but also because of the potentially catastrophic consequences of an aircraft accident. Further, federal supervision of aviation has a marked effect on aircraft safety, a factor that insurers recognize.

COMMON AVIATION EXCLUSIONS

For instance, certain exclusions appear in almost every aircraft policy. Coverage does not apply:

- to aircraft which are not registered as airworthy by the Federal Aviation Administration (FAA);
- if the aircraft is used for any purpose other than the one for which it is classified;
- if the aircraft is flown by a pilot other than one who meets rigid specifications (in some cases, a plane may be flown only by a pilot named in the policy);
- to aircraft flying in conditions requiring a special permit or waiver from the FAA, even if the permit or waiver is issued.

The market for aviation insurance includes commercial passenger and cargo airlines as well as business firms that use their own aircraft. Individual airplane owners, operators of flight schools, aircraft manufacturers and charter services are also eligible for coverage.

In the U.S., aviation policies are not standardized and are written by individual companies as well as by two large pools—the United States Aviation Insurance Group and Associated Aviation Underwriters. In addition, much aviation insurance is purchased from insurers outside the United States.

PHYSICAL DAMAGE COVERAGES

Coverage for damages to the aircraft varies among insurers. Most policies, however, separate the physical damage coverage, including crash and collision damages, into two parts—in-flight coverage and coverage for aircraft not in motion.

For the idle plane, all-risk coverage (against all perils except those which are specifically excluded) is common. For aircraft in motion, owners may purchase either all-risk coverage or coverage against certain named perils only.

Deductibles are common and generally differ for in-motion and not-in-motion coverages. Insurance for larger, more expensive aircraft may have deductibles in the thousands of dollars.

The usual aircraft policy does not cover lost profits resulting from the loss of use of an insured aircraft. However, aircraft loss-of-use insurance may be purchased as a separate coverage.

SUBSTITUTE AIRCRAFT

If substitute or non-owned aircraft are used temporarily, they are not covered under the policy. Coverage for this situation may be obtained by purchasing aircraft non-ownership insurance.

LIABILITY COVERAGES

Under aircraft liability insurance, the insurer generally agrees to pay the expenses of providing immediate medical aid at the time of an accident, of investigating accidents, of assuming the defense of suits against the policyholder, and of paying any resulting awards up to the policy limits.

The three basic liability coverages included in aviation package policies are:

AIRLINE PASSENGERS

- Passenger bodily injury. This covers the owner's liability growing out of bodily injuries or death suffered by fare-paying passengers or guests. Some policies list mental anguish as a covered bodily injury. Limits apply usually to the passenger capacity of the plane, with minimum required limits as set by state laws.
- Bodily injury (excluding passengers). This covers the aircraft owner's liability in case of bodily injuries or death to members of the public other than passengers and employees.
- Property damage. This pays for any property damage caused by the aircraft.

Other liability coverages, such as medical payments coverage, may be added to the basic policy by endorsement. Coverage also is available for damage to merchandise or baggage carried on a plane. Liability policies for airport owners, hangar keepers, and sponsors of air meets also are available.

International Flights

Aircraft accidents during international flights can present legal concerns for claimants, especially in respect to determining which country's laws apply (those of the country in which the accident occurred, or the home country of the claimant or of the airline) since the liability laws of different countries vary widely.

WARSAW CONVENTION

To clear up these concerns, an international agreement, called the Warsaw Convention, was reached in 1929 to set a limit of liability for death, bodily injury and property damages to baggage and cargo for all airlines. Persons involved in aircraft accidents during international flights could receive up to 125,000 French gold francs (the equivalent of $16,000). The airline is assumed to be liable, although the airline may challenge the assumption.

The Warsaw Convention has been amended twice since 1929. The Hague Protocol of 1955 (never ratified by the U.S.) doubled the original limit of liability. The U.S amendment, called the Montreal Agreement (1966), set an absolute limit of liability in U.S. dollars ($75,000) and eliminated the need for claimants to establish negligence of any airline with international flights originating, touching down or terminating in the U.S.

At the outset of the eighties, additional amendments to the Warsaw Convention, further raising the airlines' absolute limit of liability to about $335,000, were pending Congressional approval. The amendments also would establish a uniform international monetary exchange. The amendments, called Protocol 3 and Protocol 4, superseded changes that were proposed at a meeting of various countries held in Guatemala in 1977.

MARINE INSURANCE

Marine insurance began, as the name suggests, as insurance on ships and their cargoes against the hazards of the seas. Over the years, it has come to apply not only to ships but to almost anything that moves—and even to things that facilitate movement, such as bridges.

For many years, most transportation was by sea and by inland waterways and was insured according to time-tested marine insurance principles found in policies developed as long ago as the sixteenth century. Until the emergence of an American market, the coverage was a specialty almost totally dominated by English insurers.

The first marine insurance company in the U.S. was established in 1792, and covered the majestic American clipper ships, the jets of that era, and the cargoes they carried. That same company, the Insurance Company of North America, exists today, insuring against similar perils of the high seas—only now the coverage is for oil tankers and huge cargo ships.

When the railroad industry burgeoned, marine insurers, already experienced with transportation coverage, created policies for that industry. Even the earliest automobile property coverages were modified marine policies that applied to horse-drawn carriages.

TWO MAJOR DIVISIONS

Over time, marine insurance became a mixture of broad coverages applicable to various properties in a variety of circumstances. The expansion process began by differentiating between insurance for land and sea risks. Eventually, the term marine insurance became a general one, encompassing two more widely used insurance types. These types, still in use today, are:

Ocean marine, which covers risks whose mode of transportation is by waterways.

Inland marine, which covers transportation-related or transportable property on land.

In the U.S., marine insurance is subject to a document called the Nationwide Marine Definition—a statement meant to clarify the extent of marine insurance. Prepared by marine insurers and adopted by the National Association of Insurance Commissioners in 1933 and revised subsequently, the document enumerates the types of property for which marine coverage is applicable and property for which it is not applicable. Broadly defined, marine insurance covers such property classifications as:

NATIONWIDE MARINE DEFINITION

- import and export property in transit to its destination;
- domestic shipments during their course of transportation;
- structures and equipment relating to transportation and communication (such as bridges, tunnels, television and radio antennae);
- personal articles—such as fine art, valuables and salesmen's samples—that can be used in many different locations even though they may be at a fixed location for a period of time.

OCEAN MARINE INSURANCE

The origin of ocean marine insurance, a coverage for vessels and their cargoes on the high seas, lakes or inland waterways, is imbedded in antiquity—perhaps as far back as 3000 B.C. Some policies used today are based on a Florentine ordinance dated 1523. The evolution of the world's oldest insurance type has led to the general acceptance of a standardized insurance document.

Commercial ocean marine insurance is international in scope. Stiff competition exists among insurers in many countries; an importer or exporter may have the option of purchasing coverages from the country in which it is domiciled, a country with which it transacts business, or in some cases the country in which it does its banking.

PROPERTY COVERAGES

Basically there are two types of ocean marine property coverages—insurance for the boat or vessel, called hull insurance, and insurance for its cargo.

HULL, CARGO COVERAGES

Hull insurance can be written to cover the entire ship (less the cargo) including equipment, machinery, cranes and winches, passenger fittings, furniture and other gear. Navigation policies apply to vessels operating on the seas, while port risk policies apply to vessels docked for periods of repair or nonuse. Coverages are available for single ships or fleets, as well as large personal pleasure boats.

Cargo insurance is written as a separate coverage from hull insurance because merchants customarily ship or receive cargo via vessels owned by others. Cargo may be covered for a particular voyage, a specified time period, or until cancelled.

Insuring conditions can vary from "all-risk" to limited terms called "free of particular average" (FPA). FPA, generally, applies only to total losses unless a partial loss results from fire, sinking, stranding or collision. The term particular average is used to describe partial losses sustained by the particular interest (such as a cargo owner) involved.

PEAK VALUE FEATURE

Determining the value of vessels and cargos is critical to insurers for the purpose of establishing insurance limits and loss amounts, but often difficult for shippers during periods of high market fluctuation because values of bulk commodities may be unknown until the cargo reaches its destination. For these situations, insurers offer a peak value clause endorsement which insures the cargo for an amount equal to the peak market value of the cargo during the trip, regardless of the market value at the exact time of the loss.

For example, a cargo of wheat covered by the peak value endorsement leaves the U.S. destined for South Africa. During the trip, which normally takes 16 days, the cargo is ruined by an insured peril. Under the peak value clause endorsement, the owner is reimbursed for the loss at the top value for the commodity over that 16-day period.

Perils Covered

The ocean marine policy covers perils which are unforeseen

or accidental—collision with another ship, stranding, sea water damage, and similar occurrences. Losses resulting from such things as wear and tear, decay and leakage of liquid cargo due to faulty packaging are not covered. Also, war risk coverage generally is excluded from basic marine policies, but may be purchased by endorsement.

Among perils commonly covered are:

- Perils of the sea. This is defined as damage by wind and waves, lightning, collision, sinking, capsizing or stranding of the ship. Damage caused by sea water leakage due to one of these perils is covered also.
- Fire. Damage by accidental fire is covered whatever the cause.
- Pirates. Although the likes of Blackbeard and Captain Kidd no longer sail the seas, many policies still include the piracy provision, which relates to losses resulting from an act of violence at sea by passengers who mutiny and rioters who attack the ship from the shore.

PIRATES AND THIEVES

- Assailing thieves. While some insurers have dropped the piracy coverage, the assailing thieves provision in effect is a safeguard against this peril. It covers acts or threats of violence.
- Jettisons. This covers property thrown overboard to preserve the ship or the rest of the cargo.
- Barratry. Barratry is a fraudulent, dishonest or illegal act by the crew or captain of which the owner is unaware. Any losses from barratry, such as running away with the ship, sinking, or abandonment are covered.
- Other perils. This is not meant to be an "all-risk" coverage, but rather a protection against other perils not spelled out but similar to those already listed in the policy.

Implied Warranties

Certain provisions are included in ocean marine policies which if not respected by policyholders can void the coverage. These "implied warranties" are necessary because of the nature of operating a ship and the losses that could occur due to the negligence or irresponsibility of the captain or crew. Some of these provisions are:

- Seaworthiness. The ship must be seaworthy—able to withstand the ordinary perils of the seas—before the voyage takes place.
- Legality. Any illegal trip (for smuggling purposes, for example) can void the coverage.

- Implied warranty of no delay. On policies covering a particular trip (rather than those covering all ships and cargo during a certain time period) insurers expect the trip to commence as near to schedule as is reasonable.
- Implied warranty of no deviation. Deviations from direct or customary routes can void the policy.

Other Features

Obviously, when a ship and its cargo are imperilled at sea as a result of fire, storm or some other peril, all efforts must be made to keep the ship afloat. Often, ship-saving efforts cause losses only to portions of the ship or cargo. In order to prevent inequity, each owner assumes a share of the loss resulting to those whose property by chance is damaged or lost as a result of some voluntary action to save the entire ship. This method of apportioning losses is known as general averaging.

GENERAL AVERAGING

To illustrate, suppose cargo stored on the deck of a ship was jettisoned in order to save a ship from capsizing. Since the jettison resulted from a peril common to everyone who has a stake in the voyage, the owner of the lost cargo would not be required to sustain the entire loss; rather, each cargo owner as well as the ship owner would pay a prorated share.

Should a fire break out in the engine room, damages to cargo caused by firefighting—water, steam or chemical extinguisher—probably would be considered a general average sacrifice. Hull and cargo policies usually cover general average losses, that is, losses caused in seeking to control the fire. The actual damage caused by the fire, however, would not be considered a general average loss. It would be paid under property coverage for the cargo or the ship.

SALVAGE AWARDS

In addition, a coverage is provided to pay for costs involved in rescue efforts made voluntarily by others. Mariners have a long standing obligation to save life in peril at sea. Should rescuers, called salvors, save property on board the ship as well, they may be entitled to a "salvage" award, usually a percentage of the value of the goods and vessel saved.

Ocean marine insurance is a specialty line of insurance full of intricacies. In the international market, there is an almost endless variety of endorsements and clauses meeting virtually any situation that might arise during the time a vessel travels the high seas.

LIABILITY COVERAGES

Ships damaging other vessels and/or cargoes on board due to a negligent act of the captain or crew are covered under a collision liability coverage included in the hull policy. This same coverage protects the ship owner from liability relating to lost freight charges or loss of use costs incurred by the other ship damaged in the collision.

PROTECTION, INDEMNITY INSURANCE

To assure a more complete liability coverage, including liability arising from accidental damage to other vessels, piers, wharves, cargo on docks, or other structures or property, most ship owners purchase a policy called protection and indemnity insurance.

While this coverage usually is written separately for large commercial ships, it is combined with collision liability for large personal pleasure boats in what often is called a yacht policy.

Protection and indemnity insurance protects against most liabilities not covered by the collision clause, including the ship owner's liability to passengers, crew members and owners of the ship's own cargo.

In addition, protection and indemnity insurance provides reimbursement for fines paid to states or countries because of a violation of law, costs for disinfecting a ship, quarantine expenses and others. Protection and indemnity insurance is likened to public liability coverages for premises on land—only in this case the premises are afloat.

OIL SPILLS

The operator of every ship entering U:S. waters is required to provide proof of the ability to pay for any damages caused by pollutants, including oil spills, which might escape from the ship. A special pollution insurance policy is available for this purpose.

INLAND MARINE INSURANCE

Together, the words inland marine are a seeming contradiction in terms. Inland marine insurance has nothing to do with insuring ships or their cargoes but, instead, insures land shipments, instrumentalities of transportation and communication, and movable property—including almost anything from a suit of clothes left at the cleaners to a Picasso or a Rembrandt.

At the turn of the century, inland marine policies covered property that some fire insurance companies were hesitant to insure. Movable properties, such as tourist luggage and the samples of traveling salesmen, were among the earliest inland marine coverages. In 1912, when parcel post deliveries were introduced, inland marine insurers covered them. Soon after, because bridges and tunnels are aids to moving property, they were covered by inland marine insurers. This established the chief characteristic of the inland marine insurer, a capacity to venture into unprecedented fields of risk.

UNUSUAL RISKS

Today, inland marine provides financial protection against perils to almost anything transportable: artificial turf in sports stadiums, for example; white mice used in the space program; the beryllium nose cone of a moon rocket; or a submarine (a small one) being shipped on a flatbed trailer; even corpses.

Inland marine policies also insure railroad rolling stock and off-the-road mobile contractors' equipment, such as $2 million air cushion vehicles that snake pipelines across the Arctic tundra, 17-story cranes that help build skyscrapers and giant loaders that dig 60 tons of coal every five minutes.

Insuring unusual or even unique risks under "tailor-made" policies, at rates for which there is no guiding precedent, is commonplace for inland marine insurers. Approximately three-fourths of all inland marine premiums stem from such non-standardized underwriting, conducted in a highly competitive market.

To the insurance buyer, an attractive feature of many inland marine policies is "all-risk" coverage. This means all "fortuitous happenings": fire, theft, and many others, but not normal wear and tear or depreciation.

The five largest classes of inland marine insurance are contractors' equipment, jewelry, motor truck cargo, installations and transportation. Installation, a modest enough term by itself, often means something as significant as the construction of a power plant, an oil refinery or even a subway system.

E.D.P. INSURANCE

Electronic data processing coverage is becoming increasingly important, particularly to companies with millions of dollars worth of equipment, component parts and tapes. The four major E.D.P. coverages that inland marine writers insure are:

- data processing equipment and component parts,
- data processing media, including magnetic tapes, discs, drums and other communications forms,
- extra expenses to continue operations in the event of damage to the processing system, and
- business interruption resulting from total or partial cessation of data processing operations.

BLOCK POLICIES

One of the broadest inland marine forms is the block policy (an anglicized version of the French phrase "en bloc," meaning "all together"). The jewelers' block policy, for example, protects not only against loss of the jewelers' stock, but also against loss of the customers' jewelry if the loss occurs while in the jeweler's custody. Also covered are items on consignment from other jewelers and jewelry that is in possession of customers for approval or on-the-road with the insured's salespersons.

Similar block policies are available to furriers and to dealers selling a variety of merchandise, such as musical instruments, cameras, appliances, marine supplies, scientific and professional instruments and industrial machinery and tools.

BAILEES' CUSTOMERS

Another type of inland marine coverage—beneficial to both certain kinds of businesses and their clientele—is called bailees' customers insurance (a bailee is anyone who has temporary possession of someone else's property). This coverage is used frequently by laundries and dry cleaners and also is commonly purchased by repair shops, department stores and other merchants who have customers' goods in their custody for repairs, renovations or other services. The policy covers the destruction of or damage to such goods as a result of fire or other insured peril.

PERSONAL ARTICLES FLOATER

Perhaps the most familiar form of inland marine insurance is the personal articles "floater," which offers an opportunity to insure many valuable items in a single policy. The floater policy covers jewelry, furs, photographic equipment, musical instruments, silverware, gold, equipment, stamp and coin collections, and fine arts, and often is provided as an endorsement to a homeowners policy.

INSURANCE AGAINST CRIME

Various forms of insurance available to businesses help protect them from losses caused by thieves.

A thief's visit can go unnoticed until the loot is found missing or a trail of damaged property—such as broken glass, locks, fixtures and opened safes—is discovered. Theft policies cover both the missing goods and the damaged property. (Crime losses also are covered in all-risk property policies.)

BURGLARY, ROBBERY INSURANCE

In general, theft policies cover two types of crime—burglary and robbery. Burglary is defined as a forced entry, robbery as the taking of property from a person by force or threat of violence. Policies can be written to cover property inside a building or during its conveyance from one location to another, or both.

In addition, other crimes can be covered by endorsement to a policy if protection against them is not included in the basic policy. Some of these crimes are forgery, embezzlement, misappropriation, willful obstruction, willful misapplication and mysterious disappearance.

Commercial theft coverages fall into two general categories, those for banks and financial institutions and those for mercantile and other businesses.

BANKER'S BLANKET BOND

Many banks purchase a banker's blanket bond which covers losses from employee fraud and dishonesty as well as robbery, burglary, other crimes and mysterious disappearance (the disappearance of insured property for which there is no explanation). Thefts committed by non-employees are also covered.

Banks wishing to exceed the blanket bond's protection with higher limits of coverage may purchase a bank excess burglary and robbery policy. The excess policy offers protection against losses from burglaries and robberies of money, securities and other property and for property damage due to malicious mischief or vandalism. Unlike the banker's blanket bond, however, the excess policy does not cover employee dishonesty.

Commercial firms other than banks may purchase burglary, robbery and larceny coverage for stock, money, securities and other valuables, indoors or outdoors, in safes or other locations.

Various forms of theft coverage are available for basic or broad protection, depending upon the needs of the business. These include a money and securities policy, office burglary and robbery policy and the storekeeper's burglary and robbery policy. Commercial firms also may purchase fidelity bonds (see page 57) to protect against employee dishonesty since this coverage is excluded from some theft insurance policies.

Losses from burglary, robbery, employee dishonesty and forgery also may be covered in combination through a package policy.

3-D POLICY

One commonly-used policy is called the comprehensive dishonesty, disappearance and destruction (3-D) policy. The 3-D policy covers losses by dishonest officers and employees, theft on or off the premises, acceptance of counterfeit U.S. or Canadian currency, money orders not paid by the issuer, forgery and alteration of the business' own commercial paper. Additional coverages are: incoming check forgery; paymaster robbery; securities of lessees of safe deposit boxes; credit card forgery. Extortion coverage can be added.

KIDNAP AND RANSOM INSURANCE

In 1932, Charles A. Lindbergh Jr., 20-month-old son of the famous flying ace, was kidnapped from his Hopewell, N.J. home and murdered. The notoriety surrounding this event led to the development of a new kind of insurance—kidnap and ransom. Its purpose is to reimburse a policyholder for any ransom or extortion payments up to a certain limit, usually in the millions of dollars. Generally purchased by companies to protect key executives and sometimes other employees, the policy can cover extortions (situations where persons attempt to profit by threatening to do something or not to do something) and any payments made to secure the release of a kidnapped person. The payments may include not only the ransom but rewards and other expenses, such as the interest on bank loans taken to raise the ransom.

EXTORTION

A kidnap and ransom policy may be endorsed to cover damage done by an extortionist as a means of coercion. As an example, an extortionist might introduce a contaminant into one batch of a food product and threaten further contamination. The insurance would cover the cost of any necessary product recall as well as damages resulting from the contamination.

SURETYSHIP

The prologue to modern suretyship is buried in antiquity and is said to have begun in tribal custom. When one tribe was indebted to another, it was customary to take hostages by treaty or by force as a guarantee of payment. An unsettled debt could mean the loss of the hostages.

SURETY BONDS

PROMISE TO PERFORM

Today, suretyship works in a similar fashion—but with financial commitments in place of hostages. The surety company, in exchange for a premium, issues a bond guaranteeing to one party that another will perform specified acts—often within a stated period.

Bid bonds and performance bonds promise, for example, that a construction contract will be performed and that all suppliers will be paid. Should the contractor fail to perform as specified, the bonding company will step in and either complete the task or indemnify the person or firm for which the work is being done—up to the limit of the bond.

Without the performance guarantee of surety bonds many construction projects would never get under way or would stand half-completed.

Surety companies have carried to completion all manner of private and public works, buildings, roads, canals, railways, water works, dams, ships and utility projects.

Surety bonds are available for many situations. As examples:

- Property legally impounded during a lawsuit can be released under a surety bond guaranteeing its availability when needed.
- A liquor dealer may be required to purchase a surety bond to assure to the state payment of penalties which may be imposed for violation of the law.
- A person who is charged with a crime may be released, pending trial, under the terms of a surety (bail) bond.
- A pawnbroker or other custodian of property may be required to obtain a surety bond to protect the owners of the property from loss.

Surety bonds also serve such other purposes as protecting the helpless against wrongful acts by their guardians, guarding the taxpayer against unfaithful performances by public officials (such as theft or fraud by municipal treasurers, custodians of bond issue money or other governmental officials), and enabling plaintiffs to pursue litigation to final judgments (by guaranteeing payment of court costs).

SBA MINORITY PROGRAM

The Small Business Administration, an agency of the federal government, has developed a special bonding program to aid minority-owned contracting firms that are economically disadvantaged.

Under the Surety Guaranty Program, the SBA agrees to indemnify participating surety companies for 90 per cent of their loss costs and expenses incurred on any bid, performance or payment bonds underwritten for small business concerns acceptable to the SBA and the surety company. The surety company in turn pays SBA 20 per cent of its premium for the guarantee.

FIDELITY BONDS

Fidelity bonding is often called honesty insurance. A form of suretyship, it is a means of protection for employers against financial losses due to theft, embezzlement and other dishonest or fraudulent acts by employees.

EMPLOYEE DISHONESTY

Fidelity bonds involve three parties: the bonded employee; the surety company, which pays losses if the bond is broken; and the employer, who purchases the bond as protection against the consequences of employee dishonesty.

Fidelity bonds may be written to cover:

- a single named employee;
- several employees, listed by name in a separate schedule;
- employees occupying specific positions which are described and listed in an attached schedule, or
- all employees in a firm.

Financial institutions are among the leading purchasers of fidelity bonds, along with mercantile establishments, political subdivisions and other kinds of employers who entrust to certain employees the responsibility for handling funds, securities and other assets.

BOILER AND MACHINERY INSURANCE

Boiler and machinery insurance is a specialized line of coverage for power producing equipment in business and industry. Generally, coverage is afforded against losses resulting from the breakdown of mechanical, electrical and pressure equipment ranging from boilers to refrigeration systems, engines, compressors, pumps, motors, transformers and other machinery which generates, converts or uses power.

A boiler explosion or other equipment breakdown can have consequences other than the direct damage to the equipment itself. It may result in severe damage to surrounding property and cause serious injuries or loss of life, as well as costly disruptions of business operations.

Boiler and machinery policies cover both property and liability losses as well as the reasonable cost of making temporary repairs and expediting repair work. Property coverage is provided not only for the equipment, but also for other property of the policyholder which is directly damaged as a result of an accident.

The liability section covers the policyholder's legal responsibility for damage to property of others in the policyholder's care, custody or control. The insurer also agrees to defend the policyholder and pay all legal costs involved.

Public (general) liability policies purchased by most businesses include protection for the policyholder's liability for injuries to others than employees resulting from a boiler or machinery accident. For that reason, bodily injury liability coverage is not included in the boiler and machinery policy. It may be added by endorsement, however. A boiler and machinery policy also may be endorsed to cover:

- losses resulting from an interruption of business following an insured accident;
- losses due to spoilage of specified property, such as food and other perishables, from lack of power, heat, steam, light or refrigeration resulting from an insured accident, and
- the full cost of repairing or replacing damaged property.

INSPECTION SERVICE

Virtually all boiler and machinery insurers provide a sophisticated inspection service that not only helps to prevent accidents but also leads to improvements in standards for boiler manufacture. Some boiler and machinery insurers employ large staffs of licensed inspectors and technicians; others acquire such expertise on a contract basis. These loss prevention programs frequently include recommendations for safe operating practices, machinery maintenance advisories, and safe operating practices for policyholders.

Inspections are performed for the benefit of both the policyholder and the insurer. In fact, the perceived value of this inspection service has provided much of the motivation for purchasing the coverage. A significant portion of the insurance premium is allocated to the cost of the inspection service. One of the first organized safety movements in the United States, boiler and machinery inspection and insurance continue to be a key element in today's highly industrial processes.

GLASS INSURANCE

Comprehensive glass insurance, one of the oldest casualty lines, can be purchased as protection for windows, art glass, structural glass, leaded glass, mirrors and more. Insurers agree to replace or repair all broken glass or glass damaged by chemicals as long as the damage is not caused by war, nuclear energy or fire. Scratches and surface chippage are not considered to be breakage—the damage must penetrate the entire thickness of the glass.

In addition, insurers cover costs necessary to repair or replace damaged frames, board up openings or for other remedial measures. Some policies include the costs of replacing lettering and other ornamentation.

Usually policies are written to cover glass specifically described in the contract. However, an endorsement is available which adjusts the coverage by protecting all glass of the type described in the policy. Other endorsements are available which cover neon or fluorescent signs or stained glass in leaded sections.

Although comprehensive glass insurance may be purchased as a separate coverage, many commercial firms as well as home owners are protected against glass losses under the provisions of multiple-line package policies.

REPLACEMENT FEATURE

An unusual feature of the glass coverage is the almost universal practice of insurers to replace—rather than reimburse the policyholder for—damaged glass, lettering or ornamentation. Insurers provide this service much more promptly—often on an "on-call" basis—than most property owners could do so themselves because glass insurers have long-standing arrangements with glass firms. This quick service is particularly important to businesses whose security may be in jeopardy—such as a merchant whose goods become exposed after a storefront window has been smashed. Where the replacement glass is not immediately available, the insurer will arrange for temporary measures such as boarding over the opening.

COMMERCIAL CREDIT INSURANCE

More than 98 per cent of all transactions among commercial firms in the U.S. are on credit terms. Most of this debt is duly paid. Nonetheless, nearly every manufacturer or wholesaler trading on credit has losses every year because some debtors fail to pay their bills.

A certain amount of such loss is considered a normal, routine part of the use of credit and as such is not ordinarily insured. But ever so often a large debtor becomes insolvent or for some other reason is unable to pay, and a loss occurs that could cripple the creditor's business.

Commercial credit insurance protects manufacturers and wholesalers from these atypical credit losses by providing reimbursement for lost payments due to insolvency or default.

BAD-DEBT LOSSES

The percentage of losses considered normal is determined by the insured based on the company's experience or that of a similar business. Normally, bad-debt losses are less than 1 per cent of sales.

Unlike most insurance policies, which cover losses during the policy period, commercial credit policies can be written to cover bad debts resulting from transactions which occurred before the policy was issued.

Commercial credit insurers also provide other valuable services to policyholders. They help policyholders establish sound credit management and collection methods, provide special credit-management assistance (such as investigations, advice and other aids) and help recover sums owed by insolvent accounts.

BUSINESS INTERRUPTION INSURANCE

When a business is forced into a total or a partial shutdown because of damage inflicted by a fire, a severe storm or some other peril, the indirect consequences often can be as costly as the obvious costs involved in rebuilding, renovating or replacing the damaged property.

The potential for profits could be wiped out. At the same time, payrolls may have to be met and certain other fixed expenses may continue.

LOST INCOME, FIXED EXPENSES

Business interruption insurance is designed to fill these gaps: to reimburse the business for lost income and for continuing expenses such as payroll, mortgage or rent payments and continuing utility expenses.

While there are various types of business interruption insurance designed to meet specific needs, a condition common to them all is that insurers require diligent efforts to restore the business. Insurance payments apply only as long as it takes to repair or replace the damaged property, using ''due diligence or dispatch,'' so that business may be resumed.

Business interruption insurance offers a high degree of flexibility. There are standard forms created for the separate needs of retailers/wholesalers and service establishments and of manufacturing plants. At the same time, there are numerous versions—or related policies—designed to meet the peculiar needs of other kinds of business operations or to deal with special circumstances. As examples:

- For certain kinds of businesses, such as dairies, newspapers or clinics, it is important to continue operating regardless of the extent of damage to their property. Often, extra expenses must be incurred to relocate operations to temporary facilities, for example. An entirely separate coverage—extra expense insurance—offers reimbursement for expenses incurred in such relocations or in the use of other facilities. Some firms find it advantageous to have a combined business interruption and extra expense policy which covers both the loss of operating income and the extraordinary expenses necessary to keep the business in operation.

- Other businesses, such as restaurants or taverns, need time to re-attract clientele after they resume operation. They may purchase an endorsement to the business interruption policy extending the time period of insurance payments to cover lost profits until business is back to normal.
- Colleges and schools can purchase a special policy which reimburses them for lost tuition resulting from a circumstance covered by the policy, such as the destruction of a dormitory by fire.
- A business under construction may be prevented from opening on schedule due to damage to uncompleted buildings. Coverage may be provided for loss of earnings from the originally planned opening date until the business actually opens.
- A business may have to suspend operations because of its dependency on another firm—for parts or services or as a major customer, for example—whose business is interrupted because of fire or another insured peril. Contingent business interruption insurance offers protection against such a possibility.

CONTINGENT BUSINESS INTERRUPTION

RAIN INSURANCE

Promoters of certain kinds of events such as fairs, sports matches, or auctions have a special cause for concern—the weather. Bad weather conditions can result in a cancellation, an expensive interruption or, if nothing worse, a much lighter turnout than expected.

Rain insurance is designed to protect people who have a financial interest in an event whose success depends on favorable weather. It covers loss of income, profit or expenses as a consequence of rain, hail, snow or sleet. It doesn't cover property damage, however, or losses resulting from cold or threatening weather.

Unlike other forms of insurance, rain coverage usually is in force for only a short time, often for as little as a few hours. A rain policy stipulates that there must be at least a specified amount of precipitation before payment will be made.

Two types of rain insurance policies are available. A basic form covers actual losses caused by rain up to the policy limits. The second, called the optional form, covers the full amount of insurance specified in the policy for the particular event. An optional policy, for example, with a limit of $10,000 pays $10,000 should rain occur during the specified period. Hence, profits and expenses must be projected before purchase of the policy.

RAINFALL REQUIREMENTS

Both policies have optional minimum requirements of .05, .1 or .2 inches of rainfall. The policy provides for measurement of precipitation, usually relying on the U.S. Weather Bureau for reading. Where this service is unavailable, a rain gauge is set up and the readings are taken under the supervision of an individual agreed upon by the policyholder and the insurance company.

WORKERS' COMPENSATION INSURANCE

The industrial expansion that took place in the United States during the 19th century was accompanied by a significant increase in workplace accidents and injuries. At that time, the only way injured workers could obtain compensation was to sue their employers for negligence. For the employee, proving negligence was a costly, time-consuming effort, and often the court ruled in favor of the employer.

By the early 1900's a state-by-state pattern of legislative

proposals had begun to emerge, but it wasn't until 1911 that the first group of states enacted workers' compensation statutes. These statutes were based on the workers' compensation systems introduced in 1884 for mining industry workers in Austria and Germany, the first countries to adopt a modern workers' compensation system. The laws provided compensation to workers hurt on the job, regardless of who was at fault. Thus, the costs of medical treatment and wage loss benefits were made the responsibility of the employer.

EARLY STATUTES

As part of the compromise which made the employer liable for work-related injury and disease costs regardless of fault, the employee surrendered the right to sue at common law when the employer's negligence caused the employee's injuries.

Over the years, the compensation insurance coverage which employers provide for their workers has expanded greatly, both in terms of the number of workers covered and the quality of protection offered.

Today, all 50 states, Puerto Rico, the U.S. Virgin Islands, American Samoa and Guam have workers' compensation laws, and it is estimated that approximately 9 out of 10 people in America's work force have this protection.

EXPANDING BENEFITS

The benefits provided today are the result of many actions by state legislatures, which are solely responsible for setting benefit levels. Changes in the benefit levels in various states have been particularly rapid during the last decade. This is largely the result of a 1972 report issued by the National Commission of State Workers' Compensation Laws, which recommended, among other things, that states voluntarily make coverage compulsory and provide for unlimited medical and rehabilitation benefits, full coverage of occupational diseases and increased weekly income benefits for death and disability.

Although at the end of 1980 no state had adopted all of the 19 recommendations which the Commission termed "essential," the benefits provided to injured workers today are far more comprehensive than those which were available at the time the report was issued. These benefits can be expected to increase even more as a result of anticipated legislative action and benefit escalation clauses which are already part of state laws.

COMPULSORY ASPECTS

Workers' compensation protection is now compulsory for nearly all employees in all but three states. But even in New Jersey, Texas and South Carolina, where the laws make coverage elective, nearly all businesses provide the coverage in order to limit their risk of negligence suits.

State workers' compensation laws protect employees in nearly every occupation. The only employees for whom coverage does not apply work in job classifications which are specifically exempted by law. Workers most commonly exempted include agricultural laborers, domestic workers, casual laborers, public employees, and employees of non-profit groups and businesses which employ fewer than five persons in some states and fewer than three or less in other states.

OTHER STATUTES

Some workers not covered by state compensation laws are eligible for benefits under other statutes. The Federal Employees' Compensation Act covers employees of the federal government, the Federal Employers' Liability Act covers railroad workers and the Longshoremen and Harbor Workers' Act covers maritime workers, other than seamen. Seamen are covered under the provisions of the Merchant Marine Act.

COVERING EXCLUDED EMPLOYEES

Some states include in their workers' compensation laws coverage for farm workers or casual employees who meet certain minimum hours-worked or dollars-earned limits. Where farm workers, domestic employees and casual laborers are not covered by state laws which require workers' compensation insurance, employers may purchase the coverage on their own accord. Should a work-related injury or illness occur to an uncovered employee—one whose employer did not opt to purchase the coverage—the employee has the right to sue the employer for negligence.

BENEFITS PROVIDED

The primary function of workers' compensation is to provide benefits to the injured worker. While benefits vary from state to state, workers' compensation insurance provides coverage for the major types of financial losses—lost or reduced wage-earning ability and medical and hospital expenses. In general, the following benefits are provided:

- medical—payments for hospital, doctor and other medical expenses.
- disability—weekly payments for a portion of lost income subject to a maximum amount while an employee is disabled. Payments also are made to an injured worker when

he or she has returned to work but because of the injury has a lessened earning capability.

- rehabilitation—therapy that will enable the worker to return to the job or to train for a new position.
- survivor benefits—payable in the event of death resulting from a work-related accident or disease. Death benefits are generally paid to the spouse until remarriage and to the children until a specified age. Benefits provided include a proportion of the worker's former weekly wages as well as a burial allowance.

VARYING BENEFIT FORMULAS

State workers' compensation laws vary so that injured workers in different states, even in similar jobs or employed in the same company, do not necessarily receive identical benefits. Benefit levels set by state legislatures are based on varying formulas usually including as factors the average weekly wage for all workers in that state and the individual worker's weekly salary. Some states may include a limitation on the number of weeks they will pay for certain types of injuries.

All these factors affect the cost of workers' compensation insurance to the employer.

OPTIONS FOR EMPLOYERS

In nearly every state, before employers can commence business operations they must provide security for workers under the workers' compensation system. The following options, which vary from state to state, are available for obtaining coverages:

- Private Insurers. Coverage may be obtained either through an insurance agent or broker or directly from an insurance company. About 70 per cent of all workers' compensation insurance is purchased through the private insurance market.
- Self-Insurance. The employer itself furnishes workers' compensation benefits to the employee. This approach requires that the employer submit proof of financial responsibility to the state. To do this the employer must have—or hire—the technical expertise and staff to administer the complex compensation system, and also must deposit securities or a bond to guarantee that no single claim or series of claims would be so expensive as to endanger the payment of future claims to workers or threaten the solvency of the business.

- State Insurance Fund. An agency of the state created to provide workers' compensation insurance. There are two types of state funds:

  Competitive Funds. These funds compete with private insurance companies and self-insurers to provide a workers' compensation market within the state. At the beginning of 1980, twelve states had competitive funds. Those states are Arizona, California, Colorado, Idaho, Maryland, Michigan, Montana, New York, Oklahoma, Oregon, Pennsylvania and Utah.

  Exclusive Funds. In six states, Nevada, North Dakota, Ohio, Washington, West Virginia and Wyoming, exclusive or monopolistic state funds are the sole writers of compensation insurance. They must accept all applicants for insurance—however, this inability to select risks is balanced by the fact that the monopolistic funds can raise premiums to avert insolvency without fear of losing clients. In some states with exclusive funds, employers are permitted to self-insure.

ASPECTS OF AN EFFECTIVE PROGRAM

There are several important aspects which must be considered if a sound and effective workers' compensation program—beneficial to employees, employers and the general public—is to be maintained.

These aspects are:

- Prompt handling of claims and getting insurance money to the injured worker or, in the event of death, to the dependents, as quickly as possible.
- The establishment of services which are designed to prevent accidents and reduce losses.
- Assuring that good medical care and rehabilitation programs are available to assist injured workers.

LOSS PREVENTION

The last two points best illustrate the ongoing effort by insurers to help prevent and reduce losses in the workplace. Private insurers, for example, employ thousands of full-time occupational safety engineers, industrial hygienists and environmental health specialists who isolate work hazards and devise methods to eliminate them. Also, insurers advise policyholders on how to make their operations safer and therefore less expensive to insure.

Further, insurance industry research into workplace accidents helps companies and their policyholders recognize problem areas and address those problems with increased loss control efforts. More than 150 safety codes have been developed with the financial assistance of the insurance industry and through the commitment of time and effort of insurance company personnel.

Measures to promote workplace safety have produced a significant drop in the rate of occupational injuries and deaths over the last three decades. Between 1950 and 1979, the annual rate of occupational fatalities fell from 26.3 per 100,000 workers to 13.6 per 100,000 workers. During the same period, annual occupational injuries dropped from 3,211 per 100,000 workers to 2,374 per 100,000 workers.

REHABILITATION PROGRAMS

One way insurers help to reduce losses is through physical and vocational rehabilitation programs which produce threefold benefits: the injured worker returns to work sooner, the employer experiences a shorter disruption of the work schedule and the insurer reduces the cost of providing benefits.

These rehabilitation programs have produced ancillary benefits. For example, insurance company research intended to facilitate rehabilitation has resulted in the development of mechanical aids and artificial limbs, which not only enable injured workers to return to their jobs, but benefit other members of the public who have suffered injuries not related to their work.

SECOND INJURY FUNDS

As an incentive for businesses to hire handicapped workers, the workers' compensation system provides "second injury funds" which protect employers, and the companies which insure them, from payment for injuries which occurred before a worker is hired. If, for example, an employee who has only one functioning eye loses sight in that eye as a result of an occupational accident, a second injury fund provides money equivalent to the difference between the benefits which would be paid to a worker who loses the sight of both eyes. This procedure protects the employer from having to pay benefits for total blindness when a worker loses sight in one eye only as a result of an accident. In effect, a second injury fund covers the difference between the compensation for the second injury and that allowed for the combined disability.

For almost 70 years, the workers' compensation system has demonstrated the pervasiveness of insurance in the workplace. This system makes available to a vast majority of the workforce a high degree of medical and rehabilitative care in the event of a job-related injury or illness together with the assurance of freedom from economic hardship.

PUBLIC LIABILITY INSURANCE

Both businesses and professional practitioners such as doctors, lawyers and architects have certain responsibilities—and liabilities—other than those involving employees or the use or ownership of autos or aircraft. Two forms of liability insurance, professional liability and product liability, cover certain obligations to clients or buyers.

Businesses also face a variety of liabilities in their dealings with the public. Businesses and business owners come in contact with the public by opening their doors to the general public, or by doing business at another's home, place of business, or on public property.

LEGAL OBLIGATIONS

EXPOSURES TO LOSS

Public liabilities refer to legal obligations that if neglected or broken could require that the business or business owner pay monetary damages to another party. Some of these obligations arise from:

- The ownership and maintenance of a premises. Business owners who own or lease a building or property may be held responsible for damages if a member of the public is injured or property is damaged as a result of some unsafe condition of the business premises. If a business owner fails to replace torn carpeting, for example, and a customer trips and falls, the business owner may be held responsible if an injury results.
- The conduct of a business or an operation. A firm also may be held liable for actions of employees or owners away from the premises. An employee of a roofing contractor, for example, may drop a hammer and injure a bystander while working on a project at a location other than that of the contractor.

- The manufacture, distribution or selling of products. A manufacturer, distributor or seller of a product may be held responsible for injuries or damages attributable to the product. For example, an injury could result due to a product—such as a power saw—which was defective, improperly manufactured or designed, or because of inadequate warning about a product's dangerous qualities.
- Completed operations. The completed operations exposure applies to damages caused by faulty construction, installation, service or repair work done by a contractor, but which occurs after the work has been concluded and the contractor has left the site. This liability is similar to product liability since finished work is, in a sense, a product, and that product could cause damage even after the contractor has finished the job. To illustrate, an electrical contractor might install wiring in a commercial building to accommodate a new computer system. Negligence in the installation could cause a subsequent fire or damage to the computer, for which the contractor may be held liable.
- Work done by independent contractors or subcontractors. Generally, a person who contracts work to be done (the principal) is not held responsible for the work performed by independent contractors. However, the principal may be held liable in some cases, such as those where an independent contractor performs work for the principal which is unlawful or inherently dangerous, or where the principal exercises supervision. Insurers call this exposure contingent liability.

CONTINGENT LIABILITY

- Liabilities assumed by contract. Often, business owners assume certain liabilities expressly under contract or other agreement with some other party. In signing a lease for a warehouse, for example, a business owner may exempt the warehouse owner from liability by accepting responsibility for bodily injuries occurring on the premises. This is commonly referred to as a hold harmless agreement, in that the lessor, in this case the warehouse owner, is "held harmless" from liability.

LIABILITY PACKAGE POLICIES

Broad liability protection is available through a comprehensive package policy, or through one of several specialized packages of coverages. Also, there are policies with coverages limited to specific types of public liability.

Comprehensive General Liability

The comprensive general liability policy (CGL) is the insurance industry's answer to an increasingly complex business environment. As a package of coverages, it provides protection for most of a business's insurable liability exposures. It is referred to as general liability to distinguish it from automobile, professional and personal liability insurance, which afford liability protection against exposures of a different nature and which may be purchased separately.

Under the CGL policy, insurers agree to cover all sums up to the policy limits for which the policyholder is found legally liable because of bodily injury and property damages arising out of the ownership, maintenance or use of the premises, operations and products of the policyholder as well as liability arising from the use of independent contractors.

Coverage for contractual liabilities under the basic CGL policy is limited to leases, easement agreements (where the policyholder accepts certain liabilities when rights-of-way or power or gas lines, etc., run through the property), agreements required by municipal ordinance, elevator or escalator maintenance agreements and railroad sidetrack agreements (where a firm contracts to have rail track access on its property).

DUPLICATE BENEFITS

The CGL policy does not cover liabilities for which benefits are provided under workers' compensation or unemployment insurance laws.

The policy also excludes coverage of:

- damages resulting from the release or escape of pollutants unless such discharges are sudden and accidental.
- damage to property of others which is in the policyholder's care, custody or control. This coverage is excluded due to what insurers call the "moral hazard"—in that its inclusion could lead to fraudulent claims involving collusion. The exclusion acts as a bar, for example, to an agreement between a warehouse owner and the owner of goods accepted for storage to arrange for a convenient fire and an insurance claim, with the money later to be shared by the conspirators.
- losses resulting from the withdrawal, recall, repair, replacement or loss of use of any product of the policyholder which is already on the market.
- liability resulting from a product's failure to do what it is intended to do. Although the manufacturer of a device which is supposed to reduce the gasoline consumption of a car might be held liable if the product destroyed a motor

and caused an accident, the manufacturer would not be covered against the device's failure to improve the miles per gallon ratio.

Owner's, Landlord's and Tenant's (OL&T) Liability

This coverage protects policyholders against losses arising out of the ownership, maintenance or use of their premises. Liabilities assumed by contract, or from use of products or effects of completed business operations are not covered under this policy; however, specialized forms of OL&T policy do cover these liabilities. Medical payments coverage may be included in the OL&T policy for an additional premium.

STOREKEEPER'S LIABILITY

A form of the OL&T policy called storekeeper's liability covers liabilities of store owners. This form of the policy combines product liability and medical payments coverages. It covers the store owner's liability for others' injuries and property damage in the store and in adjoining parking areas and walkways.

Manufacturer's and Contractor's Liability

Similar to OL&T, this package policy is adapted to the risks of manufacturing and contracting firms. The coverage applies generally to locations where the insured has operations in progress. Excluded from coverage are explosion, building collapse and damage to property under the ground, as well as product and completed operations liability.

SPECIAL LIABILITY COVERAGES

Insurers also offer a variety of specialized business liability coverages, some of which can be added to a comprehensive general liability policy by endorsement. Among them:

Personal injury liability

LIBEL AND SLANDER

This covers any damages for which the policyholder is legally liable because of a harm, other than a bodily injury, sustained by another individual or organization. Such harm may result from a false arrest, detention, libel, slander, wrongful entry or eviction, or other invasion of privacy or right of private occupancy.

Liquor liability (dram shop)

In many states, statutes or common law impose certain obligations on businesses or persons who manufacture, distribute, sell or serve alcoholic beverages. These laws have the effect of holding the business liable for the unlawful sale of liquor to a minor or for damages caused by a customer under the influence of alcohol. Liquor liability insurance is designed to protect businesses which might be held responsible for damages under dram shop or common law.

Garage liability

This is a comprehensive liability package policy designed for garages, auto dealers, parking lot owners, service stations, and other automotive operations. It covers the policyholder's liability for injuries or property damages resulting from accidents on the premises or involving a product or some activity of the policyholder. The coverage may include or exclude at the policyholder's option, however, any damage to automobiles of others which are in the policyholder's care, custody or control.

Airport liability

HANGAR-KEEPER'S POLICY

This policy, similar to the garage liability policy, is available for aircraft storage or service businesses such as airports. Non-owned aircraft in the care, custody or control of the aircraft storage operation are excluded from the coverage but may be covered under a hangarkeeper's liability policy.

Contractual liability

In contrast to the limited contractual liability coverage provided in the comprehensive general liability policy, this expanded coverage protects a policyholder against losses resulting from his or her assumption of liability under any kind of contract or agreement with some other party. An example would be a contractor who accepts responsibility for any accidents which might occur during the construction of a building.

Crop dusting

With the advent of aerial application of agricultural chemicals to all kinds of crops, this interesting line of insurance emerged. It covers damage to the aircraft and offers the aerial applicator several options with regard to liability. The operator may purchase liability coverage as protection against bodily injury and property damage claims arising from accidents other than those caused by the use of insecticides or chemical sprays or dust. In addition, liability protection can be purchased to cover damage resulting from the use of insecticides only, or for damage caused by the use of other chemicals including insecticides.

PROFESSIONAL LIABILITY INSURANCE

Individuals and organizations whose services are expected to meet consistently high standards because of their status as professional practitioners in their selected fields often find that their mistakes can be costly. Professional liability insurance is designed to protect them financially from the consequences of their failure to use due care and the high degree of skill expected of a professional.

MALPRACTICE; ERRORS AND OMISSIONS

One form of professional liability insurance—medical malpractice—became the subject of widespread public attention during the 1970's because of a proliferation of lawsuits against doctors and other medical practitioners, including hospitals.

Medical malpractice, however, is only one of many professional liability coverages. Under the general heading of professional liability, insurers use two categories to classify professionals. One is malpractice liability which technically applies to those professionals whose services include touching of the body. The other is errors and omissions (E&O) coverage, for those professionals whose services usually do not involve touching of the body.

COVERAGES

Professional liability insurance protects professionals from financial losses resulting from claims, including lawsuits, against them by their clients or others. Insurers agree to cover legal expenses, court costs and, if the professional is found legally liable, any sums up to the limits of the policy that the court awards the plaintiff due to negligence, errors or omissions, or wrongful acts by a professional during his or her work.

For many of the recognized professions, there are standard policies which are designed to fit the types of services provided.

Some of these are:

- Physicians, surgeons and dentists. This single policy is appropriate for each of these professionals. Miscellaneous medical liability coverage is used for chiropodists, chiropractors, nurses, laboratory technicians, opticians, optometrists, veterinarians, technicians and other medical professionals.
- Lawyers. An errors and omissions coverage is used for attorneys. It is a broad coverage which applies to any act or omission arising out of the policyholder's work as a lawyer. It can be written for partnerships or individual attorneys.
- Directors and officers. This policy is written to cover the financial consequences of business-related negligence or wrongdoing on the part of company executives or association officers, or members of boards of directors.

OTHER PROFESSIONALS

Similar coverages are available for architects and engineers, insurance and real estate agents and brokers, fiduciaries (a person who occupies a position of trust, especially one who manages the financial affairs of another), accountants and many others. Even the most obscure or esoteric professional, such as an animal trainer, may need professional liability coverage.

COMMON POLICY CHARACTERISTICS

With nearly all professional liability policies:

- No protection is afforded against premises and liability hazards other than those to which the policyholder is exposed in the conduct of professional services.
- There is no distinction between bodily injury and property damage liability. Most insurers include coverage even for intangible damages such as mental suffering, invasion of privacy, slander, and humiliation. Damage to property of others in the custody or control of the professional also is covered.
- No other coverage can substitute for professional liability insurance, nor does this coverage overlap with any other insurance coverage.
- Since reputation is critical to the professional, insurers often specify that no claims will be settled without the consent of the policyholder.

"CLAIMS-MADE" POLICIES

Many insurers provide professional liability policies on what is called a "claims-made" basis. Under this form, only those claims which are filed against the policyholder during the policy period because of some act occurring during that period are covered. When the policy is renewed with the same insurer, however, coverage for prior acts is provided back to the date the policy was first issued.

A doctor, for example, who purchased a claims-made professional liability policy on June 1, 1979, effective through May 31, 1980, would be covered for any claim made against him or her as long as the incident occurred and the claim was filed during that 12-month period. If the policy was renewed with the same insurer for an additional year, a claim made during that additional year would be covered even if the incident had occurred during the earlier period. Any claims made in 1980 resulting from acts performed in 1976 are not covered, however.

To protect further a doctor who has had a claims-made policy and then changes insurers, retires or discontinues coverage, insurers which sell this kind of policy also offer what is known as a "buy-out" policy. This covers future claims resulting from incidents which occurred during the period the claims-made policy was in force.

THE "LONG TAIL"

The claims-made policy was created by insurers as a solution to problems sometimes associated with occurrence forms, where the coverage applies to all injuries arising out of occurrences during the policy period regardless of when the claim is made. The problem, in both professional and product liability, with the occurrence form is due to the "long tail" of claims that may result once the policy is out of force. For example, a sponge left in a patient's body after surgery may not be discovered for 10 or 12 years. This long tail makes it difficult or impossible for insurers to measure the extent of the risk.

Consider the doctor again, this time a doctor who purchased an occurrence based professional liability policy during the first year of practice, say 1955 through 1956. Even if the doctor changed companies, retired or dropped the coverage after 1956, the occurrence policy would cover all claims—as long as the doctor lived—which resulted from an act performed in 1955. This "long tail" of coverage represents a risk to insurers that is difficult to calculate—one that, until the claims-made form was developed, was reflected in professional liability rates.

PRODUCT LIABILITY INSURANCE

Since the start of the 1970's product liability has been a growing concern to manufacturing and distributive industries, insurance companies and the legal profession. There has been an increase in the volume of claims filed, the dollar awards made by the courts, and the cost of providing insurance protection.

Product liability insurance protects the maker or distributor of a product in the event he or she is held liable for compensation to a user, consumer or other person who suffers injury or loss arising from the use of that product.

Until a few years ago, product makers were held responsible only for product defects and breaches of warranty. Currently, however, the courts are holding manufacturers and vendors more strictly accountable for product-related injuries. This accountability for product safety exists even where the victim contributes to the injury through his or her own negligence and even though the product may have been in use for many years or may have been altered between the time of its initial manufacture or sale and the time of the accident.

DOCTRINE OF STRICT LIABILITY

The theory of strict liability of manufacturers for harm caused by their products received prominence when the American Law Institute in 1963 articulated the concept in a restatement of tort law (a body of law providing a person injured or harmed by the wrongful act of another with an opportunity to seek redress through the court system).

According to the restatement, the law, in effect, subjects the seller of a defective product to liability *even though* "(a) the seller has exercised all possible care in the preparation and sale of his product, and (b) the user or consumer has not bought the product from or entered into any contractual relation with the seller." For example, the seller of a defective power tool is liable for injuries caused by that tool, regardless of whether the injured person is the purchaser, the recipient of the tool as a gift, a borrower or a bystander observing the owner using the tool.

In many instances, the defense of manufacturers or vendors that the product met all known standards of safety at the time of construction or sale has been ruled unacceptable by the courts. Under this strict interpretation, companies have been held accountable for injuries to those using the product 15, 20 or more years after its manufacture or sale.

Companies hit by the deluge of suits and resulting higher insurance costs try to cope in various ways. Some manufacturers are operating without liability insurance and taking the risk of being bankrupted by large judgments.

IMPACT OF LAWSUITS

Thousands of American manufacturers, large and small, are finding that the cost of insurance covering the products they sell is a significant operating cost. Among the most affected industries are drugs, sporting goods, general aircraft, tools and various kinds of capital or manufacturing equipment. Even makers of industrial safety devices are, ironically, being affected.

MODEL UNIFORM ACT

Finding workable solutions to the product liability problem has not been easy. In late 1979, the U.S. Department of Commerce released a final draft of a Model Uniform Product Liability Act. Offered for voluntary use by the states, the Act sets standards for state product liability tort laws. The aim of the Act is to provide a fair balance of the interests of both product users and sellers and to help eliminate existing confusion about their respective legal rights and obligations.

The model law is one approach to the product liability problem. Other suggested solutions, which may be available only through legislation at the federal or state level, include:

- Placing limits on punitive damages and pain and suffering awards;
- Providing immunity from product liability suits if product designs are certified as having hazards reduced to an acceptable level;
- Setting reasonable statutes of limitations in product liability cases, dating from the time of manufacture;
- Eliminating duplication of benefits from different sources

(e.g. barring an injured person from collecting benefits from both workers' compensation insurance and product liability insurance as a result of a single accident);

- Regulating plaintiff attorneys' contingency fees (an arrangement under which an attorney collects a percentage, usually one-third, of the award);
- Establishing compulsory arbitration (an arrangement under which a settlement is sought outside the courtroom).

One answer which the insurance industry has stressed heavily is to do everything possible to assure that products are as safe as they can be. This includes developing standards for safer products, providing product manufacturers with advice on safety procedures and loss prevention programs, supporting legislation at the federal and state level to reduce the enormous legal costs of administering the product liability system and supporting legislation to make the standards of legal liability more definite, more predictable and more equitable.

ACCENT ON SAFETY

On the positive side, the product liability concern has helped to focus the attention of manufacturers on the need for increased attention to safety in design, improvement in quality control and inspection, and proper instructions and warnings to potential users.

COMMERCIAL MULTIPLE-LINE POLICIES

The term "multiple-line" is used to describe an insurance policy which combines more than one of the traditional lines, or types, of insurance. Even though these "multiple-line" policies are often called multi-peril policies, the terms are not synonymous. Any policy that covers certain properties from more than one peril, such as fire, windstorm, theft, etc., is a multi-peril policy. Multiple-line policies are multi-peril packages which include both property and liability coverages against a wide range of perils.

There are many commercial multiple-line policies on the market, each with a common purpose—to cover the major property and liability exposures faced by a business, organization, or group of businesses.

These policies are designed to meet virtually all insurance needs of typical businesses. For some specialized operations, unusual hazards may be covered separately or by endorsement to one of these package policies.

It is important to note that the insurance needs of large corporations, such as a major oil company, steel plant or auto manufacturer, are very complex. Rarely are all the coverages they require available in a single policy. In most cases, businesses such as these will have many policies, sometimes with one or more insurers, to protect themselves against their varied exposures to loss.

Business package policies may be grouped into two categories—those for small businesses and those for larger firms. Two commonly used multiple-line policies are the businessowners policy, used for small stores, offices and apartment buildings, and what insurers call the special multi-peril policy (SMP) used for insuring somewhat larger commercial firms. Though called a multi-peril policy, the SMP includes both property and liability coverages and thus is a multiple-line policy.

BUSINESSOWNERS POLICY

SMALL BUSINESS PACKAGE

The businessowners policy is a simplified language policy, like the series of homeowners 76 policies, and covers several areas of risk. It is designed for smaller businesses; those eligible for the coverage are: apartment buildings of 6 stories or less with no more than 60 units; mercantile operations in a single building no larger than 7,500 square feet or two or more buildings totaling no more than 10,000 square feet, and office buildings occupying no more than 3 stories or 10,000 square feet of floor space.

Under the businessowners policy, both the building and business personal property are covered. Businesses may be protected against certain named perils in a standard form policy or against all risks in a special form policy.

Business personal property includes the property of others held by the policyholder, improvements made by tenants, and items temporarily away from the policyholder's location. The policy also provides temporary coverage of business property at newly-acquired locations.

FULL REPLACEMENT

A feature of the businessowners policy is a provision that losses are paid on a full replacement cost basis. Thus, insurers require policyholders to insure their property for its full replacement value.

In addition to the property coverages, the policy covers loss of profits, stoppage of rental income and extra expenses resulting from damage or an interruption of business by an insured peril. Businesses have the option of purchasing protection against burglary and robbery and employee dishonesty, as well as coverage of exterior first floor and basement glass, exterior signs, and boiler pressure vessels and air conditioning equipment.

The policy also includes comprehensive liability protection and medical payments coverage for persons other than employees injured because of a business operation.

The liability section of the businessowners policy includes three specialized coverages:

- Personal injury liability—protection against kinds of harm other than physical injury, such as false arrest, slander or defamation of character;
- Host liquor liability—applicable to situations where liability results from serving liquor at functions incidental to the policyholder's business;
- Fire legal liability—coverage of the policyholder's liability, in case of fire or explosion, for damage to another person's property in the policyholder's custody or control or to another's property which is damaged by fire originating on the policyholder's premises.

SEASONAL PEAK FEATURE

Featured in the businessowners policy are several other coverages designed specifically for the small business. Some businesses have seasonal peaks, especially retail stores which may be heavily stocked during holiday seasons. Providing that policyholders insure their property for at least 100 per cent of the average monthly value of stock for the preceding year, policyholders are eligible for an automatic increase in coverage of 25 per cent during any peak season.

Another feature is an inflation provision which automatically increases the coverage on buildings by 2 per cent or more at the end of every three-month period. This protection helps the policyholder to adjust for inflation in property values without having to take specific action.

SPECIAL MULTI-PERIL POLICY

The special multi-peril policy (SMP) is used primarily for larger, more complex businesses and institutions. With the exception of farms, motor vehicle businesses, bowling alleys or very small apartment houses, the SMP can be used for almost any kind of business which doesn't require a special plan.

There are several basic differences between the SMP and the businessowners policy. The businessowners policy has a limited eligibility, determined by the building size and occupancy area of the business, but in one sense offers broader protection than the SMP in that replacement cost coverage is automatic. It is less flexible than the SMP, however, in terms of choices of coverages and the amounts of protection provided.

EIGHT PROGRAMS

The basic SMP policy is available in eight programs for different types of businesses—mercantile, office, apartment house, processing or service, institutional, motel and hotel, industrial and construction.

The eight SMP programs provide enough flexibility to meet the needs of nearly every sizeable firm. Each of the eight policies can be modified to meet particular needs.

For example, consider two motels. In addition to accommodations, one provides parking in a rear courtyard only while the other has an attended garage as well as a restaurant. The coverages these two motels might purchase in their SMP packages would be tailored to meet the differing circumstances—even though many of the basic coverages would appear in both policies.

Over the years, several SMP policies were introduced and tried in the marketplace. In 1977, a simplified SMP package was adopted to eliminate the duplication of coverages that occurred where several separate policies were purchased. With the exception of workers' compensation, automobile and surety bond coverages, all major risks are covered by the SMP policy or can be covered by endorsement to the policy.

In its basic form, the SMP policy includes four specific coverage areas.

- Property. Coverage for buildings and business personal property can be written on either a named perils basis or on an all-risk basis. In the case of rented property, the tenant is covered for losses to business personal property; the landlord, for the building. The SMP policy usually is written on an actual cash value basis; however, full replacement cost coverage may be purchased by endorsement.

Options under this section include coverages for such risks as business interruption, extra expense, glass, water damage, earthquake, sprinkler leakage and other perils. Business-owned automobiles must be covered separately.

- General (public) liability. Many of the standard general liability coverages are provided in the SMP. More specialized liability coverages may be added by endorsement.
- Crime. This section includes coverages for a wide range of crime perils such as burglary, robbery, and theft (inside or outside), employee theft, depositor's forgery and more.
- Boiler and machinery. Both direct losses and indirect losses resulting from the explosion or malfunction of any pressure vessels and machinery are covered under this section.

NUCLEAR INSURANCE

Insurance against losses resulting from nuclear accidents is provided by special insurance pools created by property and liability insurance companies. These pools have the resources to insure risks of a size which would be beyond the financial capabilities of any one insurance company.

NUCLEAR POOLS

The nuclear pools, whose history dates back to 1957, are the American Nuclear Insurers (ANI), the Mutual Atomic Energy Liability Underwriters (MAELU), and the Mutual Atomic

Energy Reinsurance Pool (MAERP). To achieve maximum insurance capacity (into the hundreds of millions of dollars), these pools combine their resources through reinsurance agreements with each other (when insuring smaller risks separately) as well as with foreign nuclear insurance pools, individual reinsurers and reinsurance syndicates.

The pools provide both liability and property coverages. The liability coverage protects the operators of nuclear facilities and their suppliers for legal responsibilities they may incur as a result of bodily injury or property damage resulting from a nuclear accident. This liability coverage has been accepted by the United States Nuclear Regulatory Commission as fulfilling the primary financial protection requirements of the Price-Anderson Act. The Act mandates that, in the event of a serious nuclear accident, losses would be compensated without the need to prove negligence or wrongdoing on the part of the nuclear facility management.

PRICE-ANDERSON ACT

The Price-Anderson Act places the limit of liability of each nuclear reactor facility at $560 million per occurrence. Payment of the first layer of any individual loss is the responsibility of the nuclear pools, whose combined dollar share for each occurrence has been rising over the years—from $60 million in 1957 to $160 million at the start of the eighties. In the event of a loss leading to claims in excess of the amount available from the pools, a maximum of $5 million can be collected—as a second layer of protection—from each operating reactor facility. At the outset of the eighties, there were 67 nuclear facilities in operation. The Nuclear Regulatory Commission (N.R.C.) is responsible for payment of any additional amount up to the overall $560 million limit.

DOLLAR LIMITS

Property insurance covers damage (up to $300 million) to the property of nuclear facility operators on an ''all-risk'' basis.

LIABILITY COVERAGES

Insurance offered by the liability pools is purchased by nuclear facility operators and suppliers to cover claims by the public for bodily injury or property damage caused by a nuclear accident. Claims are reported to and processed by the pools.

In the event of a serious accident or extraordinary nuclear occurrence, emergency plans developed by the nuclear insurance pools would operate to help provide immediate relief to victims. Under the Price-Anderson Act, claims following such an accident would be paid without regard to fault.

There are two types of coverage available from the liability pool:

- The facility form—covers a facility operator's liability for injury to the public or damage to the public's property caused by the "nuclear energy hazard." Suppliers and others who might be legally responsible for a nuclear incident at the facility automatically are afforded coverage as "additional interests" under this policy.
- Suppliers and transporters policy—covers companies which supply materials and equipment to nuclear facilities or which transport nuclear materials. Companies covered as "additional interests" under a facility form would use the suppliers and transporters policy for excess coverage.

PROPERTY COVERAGES

The pools offer property insurance for damages to the policyholder's property from the nuclear hazard as well as from the conventional perils such as fire, explosion and wind. Boiler and machinery coverage also is included. Coverages are available from the time construction on a facility begins through its operating life.

FOUR BASIC POLICIES

Four basic all-risk policies are issued by the property pool:

- Builder's risk—covers losses from a range of conventional perils during construction;
- Basic property damage—covers both conventional and nuclear perils through the operating life of a facility;
- Business interruption—covers loss of income during a shutdown due to an insured peril (available only to fuel fabrication or processing facilities which do not handle plutonium);
- Shippers and carriers transportation—covers damage to special nuclear materials during transit.

THREE MILE ISLAND

The first real test for the nuclear insurance system occurred on March 28, 1979 at the Three Mile Island Nuclear Facility near Harrisburg, Pennsylvania. Even though the first "major" nuclear accident produced no deaths, no injuries, and no damage to offsite property, representatives of the pools within a few hours were ready to handle claims out of a temporary office in Harrisburg.

Shortly after the incident occurred, Pennsylvania's governor recommended evacuation for certain persons within a five mile radius of the reactor. The pools' directors agreed to pay for the cost of evacuation because the threat of nuclear contamination existed—even though it was discovered later that whatever radiation may have escaped was not harmful.

Within six months, the pools had paid evacuation claims totaling $1,213,000 to some 3,160 claimants. In addition, they paid lost wage claims to 615 persons in the amount of approximately $90,000. They also incurred losses totaling $300 million to cover property damage to the facility resulting from the accident.

TITLE INSURANCE

When land changes hands in the United States, a deed is recorded. By law, mortgages, judgments, wills, certain court proceedings, taxes, assessments and other legal instruments affecting the title (documentation) of ownership are recorded also. These records are public notice that a claim exists against the land, and the owner or purchaser is subject to these claims.

THE SEARCH FOR DEFECTS

The risk involved in a title transfer results from not uncovering title defects from the multitude of records kept in a variety of places. The records include thousands of volumes and hundreds of legal instruments—all of which could have a bearing on the validity of a title.

Before 1876, when the first title insurance company was organized, most property purchasers hired lawyers to examine a title. The lawyer searched the title and certified it as good (or otherwise) in his or her legal opinion. If the opinion proved wrong, the title holder had no security against a claim to the property.

Suppose, for example, that the title to a piece of property

was sold by a person who owed a large amount of money to a creditor, say a bank, which had obtained a judgment and filed an attachment against the owner's property. Although the purchaser of the title was unaware of the judgment, he or she would stand to lose the investment if the creditor then exercised its right to take over the property to help satisfy the debt.

Title insurance protects purchasers of real estate against losses resulting from previously existing defects in a title such as unsatisfactory liens and mortgages, forgeries, misrepresentation or invalid wills.

TITLE PLANTS

By law, in many states, title insurers must maintain a complete title plant—a place where records needed to establish the credibility of a title are kept. Insurers have these title plants located in the districts where they write policies. Records are collected from governmental subdivisions, courts and the federal government—and any other source of information which could affect the title.

Through these plants, title insurers research all aspects of a title before they issue a policy. Any defects they discover which increase the chance of loss may be specified in the policy and excluded from the coverage. Once the policy is issued, the insurer assumes all losses, up to the limit stated in the policy, that result from title defects the insurer failed to find.

The policy covers only defects which existed at the time of its issuance, not those which might occur later. However, the policy is in force for as long as the policyholder and his or her heirs maintain ownership.

In addition to covering losses resulting from title defects, the insurer agrees to defend the policyholder against lawsuit involving the title. Further, the coverage makes the title more readily saleable and facilitates the borrowing of money. Title insurance frees the seller and the buyer of property, as well as the lender of money, from worries about possible losses resulting from defects or faulty examinations of titles.

SURPLUS AND EXCESS LINES INSURANCE

Nearly all of the insurance coverages needed by individuals, businesses and other institutions are available from the many companies which have been licensed by a state insurance department to do business in the state. (A company licensed to do business in a state is called an ''admitted'' company.) Typically, this protection is provided in standard insurance policies and at prices which are subject to regulation by individual states. Sometimes, however, an unusual need arises or someone wants insurance coverage for an unusual situation. In such cases, insurance companies doing business in a particular state may be unable to fill the need.

NON-ADMITTED MARKET

Just such a need occurred in the late nineteenth century when the fire insurance companies in one state were unable to meet the demands for fire insurance by a fast-multiplying number of commercial and industrial firms in the state. The firms remedied their problem by looking elsewhere—to ''non-admitted'' insurers which were willing to handle the ''surplus'' business.

Today, the term surplus lines has come to be applied to any insurance coverage (seldom as common as fire insurance, however) which is unattainable through a company licensed in the applicant's state and is obtained through a market outside the state.

Because the New York Insurance Code refers to brokers who are eligible to handle non-admitted business as ''excess lines brokers,'' the term ''excess lines'' has come to mean virtually the same thing as surplus lines. Terminology relating to this type of insurance is confused further by the fact that some companies have ''special risks'' departments which they refer to as ''surplus lines,'' ''excess lines'' or ''surplus and excess lines'' departments

SURPLUS LINES LAWS

Recognizing the need for alternate or supplemental sources of insurance under certain conditions, every state has established a surplus lines law designed to provide orderly access to and functioning of the non-admitted market.

Although the laws vary among the states, usually certain conditions must be met before business may be placed with non-admitted insurance companies. Some of the more common conditions are:

- That a diligent effort be made to place the insurance with an admitted company. While there is no uniform definition of what constitutes a diligent effort, most consider such an effort to have been made when an application for insurance has been declined by 3 to 5 admitted insurers;
- That if one or more state-licensed insurers are willing to handle a portion of the required coverage, only the amount in excess of that portion may be placed in the non-admitted market;
- That non-admitted companies cannot charge a lower rate than the lowest rate acceptable to an admitted company.

SURPLUS LINES MARKET

FOREIGN, ALIEN INSURERS

Two types of insurers make up the surplus lines market place, foreign and alien insurers. Foreign insurers is the term used for United States-based companies which handle business in states other than states in which they are licensed. Alien insurers are chartered in a foreign country but do business in the United States.

Companies dealing with surplus lines, generally, are not regulated in the same way or to the same extent as companies which are licensed to do business in the state. They have a great degree of pricing freedom and their policies do not have to be approved in advance by any state regulatory agencies.

Modern use of the surplus lines market is confined, generally, to risks:

- Of an unusual nature. Exotic risks such as the valuable pitching arm of a major league baseball player may require an amount of speculation that admitted insurers may be unwilling to make. Historically, much of this type of business has been written by insurance entities located outside of the United States, of which Lloyd's of London traditionally has been the leader.
- Which require a special form. In some cases, requirements

relating to policy forms are relatively rigid. Insurance buyers wishing to make substantive changes in the conditions of a policy may seek coverage outside of their state if the policy form they desire is not acceptable to their state's insurance department or is not available through insurance companies in the state.

- Which are substandard. When the highest rates a regulator will approve for a line of insurance are unacceptable to admitted insurers, the risk may seek coverage in other markets.
- With high loss potential (large capacity risks). The amounts of coverage needed by some types of endeavor may exceed the amount that admitted companies are able to provide. In general, these include liability risks associated with large bridges, tunnels, dams, aviation risks and large world-wide operations. In some cases, admitted insurers provide an initial layer of coverage, and the excess is provided through the surplus lines market.

BROKER REQUIREMENT

The surplus lines laws of each state provide for specially-licensed surplus and excess brokers, some of whom may be representatives of a non-admitted insurer. Typically, an insurance agent or broker who is unable to find insurance coverage for a customer in the normal market will seek the assistance of one of these brokers. In cases of very large risks, such as a major corporation, representatives of the firm may meet directly with representatives of the surplus lines insurer.

In an increasingly complex society, the use of the surplus lines market can be expected to grow. Today, more insurance companies both in the United States and throughout the world are being created to meet special needs resulting from changing technologies and customer desires. Since companies of this type usually will not have a large volume of business in each state, it is difficult and expensive for them to seek licenses in each state; instead they operate through the surplus and excess lines market.

RISK MANAGEMENT

Businesses and industries always have had to face up to the prospect of unexpected losses, from fire or windstorm, from burglars and shoplifters, from mechanical breakdowns, or from countless other sources.

As business has become increasingly vulnerable to such losses, partly because of society's growing tendency to hold it accountable for injuries suffered by employees, customers and guests alike, efforts to identify and deal with their underlying causes have developed into a new specialty—risk management.

While numerous small business entrepreneurs may have to make their own risk management decisions, often with the professional assistance of their insurance agents and brokers, many businesses have made risk management a high level staff function. Its dual goal is to minimize both the chances that a loss will occur and the financial impact of losses which cannot be prevented.

IDENTIFYING THE RISKS

RISK ANALYSIS

A major responsibility of the risk manager is to identify and evaluate the wide variety of conditions and circumstances which can lead to costly losses. This involves seeking answers to such questions as: What could cause a loss here? From past experience, what types of losses are re-occurring? How serious have past losses been? What is the potential for serious losses in the future?

To help answer these questions, many risk managers use standardized ''risk analysis'' questionnaires, often with the assistance of an insurance agent or broker.

These questionnaires take into account the potential for:

- property losses;
- business interruption losses;

- liability losses;
- losses resulting from employee injuries in the workplace, and
- key person losses (where the loss of certain employees or owners due to death, disabling injury or illness, or resignation may result in major financial problems for the business).

The risk manager is also responsible for finding ways of minimizing losses and paying for those which can't be avoided.

There are many precautions that can be taken against fire, for example, but no guarantees that a fire won't occur. Thus, the risk manager's responsibility will go beyond the practice of good fire prevention techniques—to such measures as the installation of automatic sprinklers and other fire fighting devices, to evacuation planning, even in some cases to an on-premises fire department.

The risk manager may advise, because of an identified potential for loss, that a new building not be purchased, that a proposed manufacturing process be rejected or that additional safeguards are needed on existing equipment. Or the manager might come up with a whole new security system to put a halt to an epidemic of thievery.

Governmental regulations calling for warning labels on certain kinds of products may come within the domain of the risk manager, as may the entire gamut of requirements of the Occupational Safety and Health Act.

To fulfill this wide variety of obligations, the risk manager works closely with the company's employees from management to the assembly line, as well as with government regulators, bankers, lawyers and insurance people. A thorough knowledge of the firm's operations must be supplemented with a clear comprehension of the legal and social environment in which the business operates.

DEALING WITH RISK

COST CONTROL

Since the potential for loss cannot always be controlled, the manager must take the major step of anticipating how the business will handle the costs of losses. Most firms, working with agents or brokers, purchase insurance carefully tailored to meet their specific needs at the most reasonable cost. To keep that cost down, the risk manager must determine how much of the risk the firm should assume itself through the use of an appropriate deductible.

The manager, in some cases, may decide that the company should establish a special self-insurance fund to cover a substantial first layer of any loss, with insurance coverage to pay for losses in excess of that layer. As an alternative to a self-insurance fund, some corporations opt to form their own insurance companies which insure certain aspects of those corporations' risks.

The risk manager usually augments his or her own efforts by making use of the loss control and prevention services often provided by insurers. Many insurers have loss control departments staffed with engineers and safety specialists who can help reduce losses and thus lower insurance premiums. Some kinds of insurance policies, such as boiler and machinery, provide for periodic inspections by the insurer, whose certification is accepted in fulfillment of the requirements of the many cities which mandate certificates of inspection of steam boilers.

SPECIALIZED SERVICES

Because the risk management process is influenced by factors which are constantly changing, a procedure which is important today may turn out to be inadequate tomorrow. Constant evaluation and review are important aspects of every risk manager's job.

HOW INSURANCE OPERATES

THE INSURANCE MARKETPLACE

Just as people buy other products locally, most Americans, in shopping for the various kinds of property and casualty insurance, deal directly with an insurance representative who lives and works in or near their own community and who often takes an active part in civic and other community affairs. Some companies sell insurance by direct mail.

AGENTS AND BROKERS

It's the job of the insurance agent or broker (often referred to in the business as a producer because he or she "produces" insurance sales) to advise the purchaser, to issue or arrange for the issuance of the policy, and to provide follow-up service as needed.

The buyer may choose to deal with:

- An independent agent, who usually represents more than one company;
- An exclusive agent, who is an employee or a commissioned representative of a single company;
- A solicitor, an agency employee who may make sales and collect premiums, but whose authority stops short of issuing or countersigning policies;
- A broker, who represents not the company, but the customer. The broker deals with either agents or companies in arranging for the coverage required by the customer.

COUNTER-SIGNATURES

Agents have the authority not only to sell insurance and collect premiums, but to issue or countersign policies. (While policies bear the signatures of officers of the issuing company, many states have laws requiring that policies issued in the state also be signed—or countersigned—by a resident agent or other representative of the insurer).

KINDS OF COMPANIES

Although many people tend to think of insurance as one giant industry, the private insurance business in fact is segmented in various ways. The two principal segments of the total private insurance industry—life insurers and property/casualty insurers—market entirely different products, although often companies from both segments have common ownership. An important common denominator is that their products, in the long run, are designed to provide members of the public with financial safeguards of one kind or another. Often, the same agents or brokers handle both forms of insurance.

MARKET SEGMENTS

Still other companies sell accident and health insurance exclusively, although many life insurers and property/casualty companies also compete in the accident and health market.

In a business which is heavily competitive, insurers are capitalized and operate in a variety of ways. The principal categories of companies are:

- Capital stock companies, which are owned by stockholders whose invested funds enable a company to (1) begin operations and (2) enlarge its capacity to serve the insuring public. A stockholder-elected board of directors, together with officers elected by the board, make and oversee the implementation of policies aimed at meeting the company's responsibilities to the public it serves and at achieving a profit.
- Mutual companies, which are owned by their customers, or policyholders. The policyholders elect members of the board of directors who in turn appoint officers to operate the company. The policyholder's financial "investment" is in the form of the premium he or she pays for insurance coverage, and is not to be compared with the investment of a stockholder whose aim is to achieve dividends or a profit. In some cases, depending upon operating results, a mutual company may return to its customers a payment in the form of a policyholder's dividend. (For some lines of insurance, particularly workers' compensation, a stockholder-owned company also may pay dividends to policyholders).

POLICYHOLDER DIVIDENDS

- Reciprocal exchanges, non-profit organizations through which people pool their individual risks and share them proportionately. Each subscriber's premium is recorded in a separate account, from which the subscriber's share of each loss is paid. Unlike mutual companies which are incorporated, reciprocal insurers are unincorporated organizations of "subscribers" who insure each other. A reciprocal is managed by an attorney-in-fact who may be an individual or a corporation with stockholders.

- Lloyds associations, unincorporated organizations of individuals who accept a specific portion of liability under each policy issued. American Lloyds are named after but have no connection with Lloyd's of London, the world's largest firm of individual underwriters, and comprise only a minuscule part of the property/casualty insurance market in the United States. Each Lloyds association is administered by an attorney-in-fact, and much of the risk is reinsured by other insurance companies.

CAPTIVES

In recent years, many corporate enterprises have turned to what is, in effect, a form of self-insurance through the use of "captive" insurance companies.

Basically, the captive insurer concept involves an arrangement by which a firm with a sizeable potential for certain kinds of losses buys or forms its own insurance company to take care of at least a portion of its insurance needs. While some firms decide to assume their own risks, often through the creation of self-insurance reserve funds from which losses may be paid as they occur, others perceive greater advantages in forming or participating in captives.

EXTENSION OF SELF-INSURANCE

In some cases, captives are created by and serve several corporations or organizations—often from the same industry—having similar insurance needs.

Captives usually are formed to provide the parent corporation or groups of sponsors with forms of insurance—such as product liability or workers' compensation—which they may find it more expedient to handle on their own because of cost considerations or a lack of adequate availability from standard insurance sources.

Among the incentives frequently cited for the formation of captives are: cost savings (through tax incentives, reduced premiums and lower overhead costs); direct access to the reinsurance market; improved cash flow by retaining access to reserves for investment purposes, and the development of a needed insurance market.

Large corporations often take the captive insurer route as a means of accommodating not only their own needs, but those of subsidiary companies around the world.

A majority of captives are domiciled outside the United States, a preponderance of them in Bermuda, which offers, among other things, tax advantages and less rigid regulatory requirements than those of the states. There are no income or capital gains taxes in Bermuda, and federal income and capital gains taxes are deferrable until earnings are brought back into the United States.

In the United States, Colorado in 1972 and Tennessee in 1978 enacted legislation providing incentives for the formation of captive insurers in those states. In Colorado, whose law is similar to that of Tennessee, a captive is subject to a 1 per cent premium tax but no federal excise tax. Although the minimum capitalization of $75,000 is higher than that of Bermuda, it may be established with a letter of credit rather than cash. The acceptability of a captive in Colorado is conditioned on a showing that adequate insurance markets are not otherwise available in the United States or that the coverage needed is obtainable only at excess rates or with unreasonable deductibles.

INSURANCE POOLS

Some of the underwriting operations of many insurance companies are administered by company-owned organizations which usually specialize either geographically, in one or more lines of insurance or in providing services to certain kinds of risks.

MANAGEMENT GROUPS

Many insurers which are active in other countries, for example, are members of management groups or pools, which serve as the foreign department of those companies.

One such pool is AFIA Worldwide Insurance, which serves as the foreign department of a group of capital stock insurance companies to provide American and overseas business interests with insurance services and protection throughout the free world.

Other groups, on behalf of companies which subscribe to their services, specialize in the underwriting of such highly technical lines as aircraft, ocean marine and nuclear insurance. This type of facility is typified by the three pools, American Nuclear Insurers, the Mutual Atomic Energy Liability Underwriters and the Mutual Atomic Energy Reinsurance Pool, which provide property and liability insurance protection to the nuclear energy industry.

A combination of underwriting, engineering and loss prevention services is provided by other company-owned organizations such as the Factory Mutual System and Industrial Risk

Insurers, both of which provide specialized insurance and fire protection services to risks which require a high degree of loss control.

Also falling into the category of shared risk mechanisms are the FAIR plans, beach and windstorm plans, and automobile assigned risk plans discussed elsewhere in this book.

EXCHANGES

Early 1980 saw the birth in New York City of a facility envisioned as a major competitor of Lloyd's of London in the international insurance market. The New York Insurance Exchange was established to write reinsurance of all kinds and direct insurance on risks located outside the United States as well as on domestic risks which have been rejected in what is called the New York Free Trade Zone.

FREE TRADE ZONE

The philosophy behind the formation of the NYIE was to help stem the outflow of premium dollars abroad, especially to London, where an extensive market traditionally has been available for large and unusual risks. The ultimate goal is to provide increased capacity in the U.S. insurance market for the growing demand for insurance both in this country and elsewhere.

The Free Trade Zone was created in New York to handle insurance on an unregulated basis for extraordinary or hard-to-place risks. An extraordinary risk in this case is defined as one which generates a premium of more than $100,000 for a single kind of insurance or more than $200,000 for more than one kind.

In addition, more than 200 categories of risks are identified as being eligible for placement in the Free Trade Zone. These risks are of an unusal nature, such as liability insurance for hang gliders or "crop insurance" for catfish farms. These risks rarely generate the large premium required for placement of other risks in the Zone, but because of the possible difficulties of handling them through the standard insurance market, they are accepted in the Zone.

UNDERWRITING SYNDICATES

The exchange is composed of underwriting syndicates which provide the coverages, and broker members who place the business with the syndicates. Each syndicate is made up of a managing partner and several other partners who can be insurers, representatives of foreign interests or even individuals.

As the New York Insurance Exchange began operations, additional exchanges were in the formative stages in Illinois and Florida.

REINSURANCE

Reinsurance can be described as the insurance which insurance companies buy to protect themselves against losses. Based on the same principle as insurance itself, reinsurance is a mechanism to provide for a further sharing of the risk to help insurance companies meet their obligations to policyholders. By reinsuring a portion of its risks, an insurer assures itself of the availability of funds to pay for unusually large losses or an unusually large number of smaller losses. Reinsurance may be purchased on a facultative or a treaty basis.

Facultative Reinsurance

Under the facultative—individual risk—basis, each risk which an insurance company wishes to reinsure is reviewed by the reinsurer which has the option of accepting (with or without modifications) or rejecting it.

A hospital, for example, may want coverage into the millions of dollars—more than a single insurance company may wish to accept. Rather than rejecting the application, the insurer will determine how much of the coverage it is willing to insure, then shop around for a reinsurer to accept the balance of the risk in return for a portion of the premium paid by the hospital.

This form of reinsurance is called facultative reinsurance because the reinsurer retains the "faculty" to accept or reject all or part of any risk offered to it.

Treaty Reinsurance

There are several types of reinsurance treaties, each of which falls into one of two broad categories, pro-rata and excess. Under pro-rata treaties, sometimes referred to as proportional reinsurance, the amount of insurance, the premium and losses are shared by the primary insurer and the reinsurer in agreed proportions. Under excess, or nonproportional, treaties, the reinsurer's responsibility for the payment of a loss begins only when the loss exceeds the amount of the primary, or ceding, company's retention. While either kind of treaty may be used to reinsure either property or liability coverages, reinsurance for liability almost always is written on an excess basis.

PRO-RATA TREATIES

There are two types of pro-rata treaties:

- Quota share treaty. Under this agreement, every risk accepted by the primary insurer within the class or classes of insurance subject to the treaty is shared by the reinsurer on a straight percentage basis. If, for example, a company has a 60 per cent quota share agreement with a reinsurer, the company retains (will pay) 40 per cent and the reinsurer will pay 60 per cent of any losses subject to the agreement in return for a similar portion of the premium received from the risks.

- Surplus share treaty. In this case, the primary insurer's retention is stated as a dollar amount, rather than as a percentage. The primary insurer, for example, may decide to accept full responsibility for any policy providing up to $20,000 of coverage. If the total amount of coverage of a given policy is greater than $20,000, the amount in excess of $20,000 is ceded automatically to one or more reinsurers which then share in the premium and share in the payment of any loss in proportion to their share of the policy limit.

The table below illustrates how a surplus share treaty would apply to three different policies, assuming a retention of $20,000 by a primary insurer having surplus share treaties with Reinsurers A and B, each with a reinsurance limit of $100,000.

LAYERS OF COVERAGES

While many surplus share treaties involve only one reinsurer, this example illustrates how such treaties may be built up in layers. In this case, the first layer of reinsurance coverage (up to $100,000) is provided by Reinsurer A, with Reinsurer B becoming involved only when the amount of insurance on a single risk exceeds $120,000 (the $20,000 retained by the primary company plus the $100,000 of coverage provided by Reinsurer A). In some cases, additional layers may be needed.

POSSIBLE APPLICATION OF A SURPLUS SHARE TREATY

	Total	Primary Insurer	Reinsurer A	Reinsurer B
Policy 1				
Insurance limit	$15,000	$15,000 (100%)	$0	$0
Premium	150	150 (100%)	0	0
Loss	10,000	10,000 (100%)	0	0
Policy 2				
Insurance limit	$80,000	$20,000 (25%)	$60,000 (75%)	$0
Premium	800	200 (25%)	600 (75%)	0
Loss	12,000	3,000 (25%)	9,000 (75%)	0
Policy 3				
Insurance limit	$180,000	$20,000 (11.1%)	$100,000 (56.6%)	$60,000 (33.3%)
Premium	1,800	200 (11.1%)	1,000 (55.6%)	600 (33.3%)
Loss	90,000	10,000 (11.1%)	50,000 (55.6%)	30,000 (33.3%)

As the nomenclature suggests, excess treaties provide for reinsurers to pay only the amount of any given loss in excess of the amount the primary insurer agrees to retain. There are three general types of excess treaties:

- Per risk excess. Under this kind of treaty, the primary insurer agrees to pay a certain dollar amount of any loss sustained by an individual risk and the reinsurer, subject to the terms of the agreement, is liable only for the portion of the loss which exceeds that amount.
- Per occurrence excess. This kind of treaty, sometimes known as a catastrophe treaty, is designed essentially to help primary insurers cope with unusually large losses resulting from a single occurrence such as a hurricane or a tornado. Often, such an occurrence causes widespread damage to many insured properties. While the strict definition of a catastrophe may differ from one treaty to another, this kind of agreement operates in such a way that the primary insurer agrees to pay all of the losses until the total reaches a certain dollar amount, at which point the reinsurance comes into play.
- Aggregate excess. This type of treaty provides for the reinsurer to pay only when the primary insurer's cumulative losses over a stated period of time, usually a year, exceed a specified amount.

EXCESS TREATIES

Reinsurance treaties may be written with provision for what are known as special acceptances. In such cases, the primary insurer confers with the reinsurer as to the acceptance of specific, unusual risks. Once the risk is accepted, however, the reinsurer complies with the guidelines of the treaty which establishes the arrangement in detail.

Reinsurance Pools

Another method of reinsuring is by a pooling arrangement among insurers writing similar coverages, usually those which have large loss potentials, such as aviation or workers' compensation insurance. Pools work in two ways. First, each member of the pool may assume a certain percentage of every loss. A 50-member pool, for example, might have a member with a policyholder who suffers a $100,000 loss. Each member would accept an equal portion—say 2 per cent or $2,000—of the loss, depending upon the agreement.

A second method is similar to the excess loss treaty. Each member of the pool assumes the responsibility for its own losses below a certain amount. Any losses exceeding that amount are shared by all members of the pool.

Regardless of the method used to determine the transfer of risk, the primary insurer pays a premium in return for the reinsurance protection. The amount of the premium, of course, depends on the degree of risk involved.

Insurance consumers are not directly affected by the existence of reinsurance. The primary insurer still handles all matters relating to claims and servicing and is not relieved of these obligations by the existence of reinsurance. Therefore, consumers typically do not know about and need not be concerned with reinsurance transactions.

ROLE OF REINSURANCE

However, the existence of reinsurance does provide benefits to consumers. Any insurance company would find it difficult to do business without reinsurance. It would be restricted as to the dollar amounts of coverage it could provide on a particular building or other risk. In addition, small companies, particularly those writing in small geographic areas, could have a catastrophic exposure from such events as hurricanes and tornadoes. Without reinsurance, those companies would have to restrict their writings in a given community. Reinsurance, on the other hand, provides to insurance companies the same freedom from catastrophic loss that primary insurance provides to individual consumers.

GOVERNMENT INSURANCE PROGRAMS

The Federal Insurance Administration offers three congressionally mandated property insurance programs. In addition, the federal government offers insurance on growing crops (discussed on page 38).

Flood Insurance

Owners of properties located in many areas which are vulnerable to flooding and mudslides may obtain insurance against flood and mudslide losses from the government under a program established by the Flood Disaster Protection Act of 1973. Flood insurance on fixed property is not offered by private insurance companies because it does not lend itself adequately to the fundamental risk-sharing principle. Although floods often cause widespread devastation, many areas are not subject to flooding and property owners in those areas would have no need for the coverage. Therefore, those who buy this insurance are those most likely to be flooded, which makes it uneconomical for private insurers to offer this coverage.

Flood insurance is available to owners of both residential and business properties in areas of every state, the District of Columbia, Puerto Rico and the Virgin Islands. The coverage is available to property owners only in communities which qualify by adopting and administering flood plain management programs which are intended to protect new construction from future flooding. Some 20,000 locations around the country are considered to be flood-prone, and a vast majority have qualified for flood insurance.

CONDITIONS OF ELIGIBILITY

A community's qualification for flood insurance actually is a two-step process. Eligibility for an emergency phase of the program involves the adoption of preliminary flood plain management measures. When the Federal Emergency Management Agency has completed a detailed survey which establishes flood levels, a community may move into FIA's regular program by adopting a more comprehensive flood plain management plan.

In communities which qualify for the emergency program, owners of one-family homes may buy up to $35,000 of coverage and owners of other kinds of residential structures may purchase up to $100,000 of coverage. Up to $100,000 of coverage also is available to small businesses and other non-residential structures. The contents of a home may be insured up to $10,000; of any other eligible building, up to $100,000.

Under the regular program, single-family homes may be insured up to $185,000; other residential structures and small businesses up to $250,000, and other nonresidential structures, up to $200,000. Limits of coverage for contents are $60,000 for homes, $300,000 for small businesses and $200,000 for other eligible buildings.

Every flood insurance claim payment is subject to a $200 deductible, applied separately to a building and its contents.

Although flood insurance policies are provided by the government, they may be obtained from any licensed property insurance agent or broker.

Crime Insurance

Because of severe crime problems which exist in some areas, insurance against losses resulting from burglaries and robberies sometimes is not readily available through the private insurance market. To fill the gap, Congress created a Federal Crime Insurance Program which became operative in 1971. Only those states in which the federal insurance administrator determines that an availability problem exists are eligible for inclusion in the program.

Under the program, insurance against burglary and robbery losses is offered in many states as well as in the District of Columbia and Puerto Rico. Households may purchase up to $10,000 of coverage and businesses up to $15,000, subject to deductibles. To qualify for federal crime insurance, home owners, tenants and business owners must have or install security devices meeting government specifications.

SECURITY REQUIREMENT

Federal crime insurance, where it is available, is sold by licensed property insurance agents and brokers.

Riot Reinsurance

This program provides for a federal government backup for private insurance companies which participate in state FAIR Plans, the facilities established to provide property insurance in some states to persons who have difficulty obtaining it through regular channels. This is accomplished through the sale to private insurers of government reinsurance against abnormally high property insurance losses caused by riots and other civil commotion.

Riot reinsurance is available, however, only in some of the states which have FAIR Plans. The cost of insurance purchased through some of the FAIR Plans is higher than the cost of the same coverage in the regular market. Where that is the case, under a 1979 amendment to the FAIR Plan law, insurance companies are not eligible to purchase the federal reinsurance backup.

INTERNATIONAL INSURANCE

The United States is preeminent in the world insurance market. In terms of domestic business alone, it accounts for more than three times as many premium dollars as Japan, the second ranking country. In addition, U.S. companies are active in insurance markets abroad—where they write more than $4 billion in premiums.

MEANS OF U.S. PARTICIPATION

Some individual U.S. companies operate by becoming licensed to do business in foreign countries. Sometimes the insurer files directly for a license under its own name, but the more common method is for the U.S. firm to acquire an interest in a licensed company native to another country. This eliminates problems often faced by an insurer trying to obtain a foreign license, and problems that occur when a country has laws restricting the business of foreign insurers.

ACQUIRING OVERSEAS INTERESTS

A variation of the first method is for several U.S. insurers to establish an entity to represent each company in its foreign operations. An example is AFIA Worldwide Insurance, a nine-member pool formed more than 60 years ago, which serves as each member's foreign department in the underwriting of risks on business overseas. AFIA, with 250 branches, is licensed—either under its own name or under the name of one of its members—in each of the nations in which it operates. In addition, the pool owns locally-established insurance companies in more than two dozen countries.

Reinsurance is another method by which American insurers can participate in business abroad without the necessity of being licensed in another country. A local insurer, writing a policy in its own country, can reinsure it in the United States with an American company or companies. Advantages are that the policyholder deals with a fellow countryman, the policy is serviced locally, and the need to cope with restrictive insurance laws is avoided.

Some U.S. companies participate in international business by co-insuring an overseas risk with a foreign insurer: each of two or more companies assumes a share of the risk as a primary insurer. This is a more direct way of doing business than is reinsurance, but it does require that the insured deal with (and reach agreement with) more than one insurance company on contract terms.

Also, an American insurer might have a working relationship with a foreign insurer. A policy written in the United States for an American firm on its business overseas is serviced by a cooperating insurer in the foreign country which handles, for example, claims matters.

Still another method in which the U.S. insurance industry

participates in the overseas market involves a U.S. firm owned by a foreign parent. The U.S. branch thus has access to the overseas network of its parent and can write insurance policies in countries in which the parent already is licensed.

POLITICAL RISK, EXPORT CREDIT COVERAGE

Another aspect of international insurance involves a broad category which includes political risks and export credit insurance. Most American businesses with foreign operations buy insurance to protect themselves against a variety of contingencies which may have an adverse effect on their dealings in other countries. These include war and insurrection, inconvertibility (blockage of transfer) of funds overseas, expropriation by foreign governments, and failure of a foreign purchaser to pay for cargo exported from the United States.

INSURER-GOVERNMENT PARTNERSHIP

The Foreign Credit Insurance Association (FCIA), in which more than 50 private insurance companies participate, works in partnership with the Export-Import Bank of the United States in providing export credit and political risk insurance for United States exporters of products and services. The Export-Import Bank is an independent government agency whose primary objective is to provide export financing support for U.S. exporters seeking to market their products overseas.

Insurance written by FCIA protects exporters against the failure of foreign buyers to meet their credit obligations for either commercial or political reasons.

Other kinds of protection are offered by the Overseas Private Investment Corporation (OPIC), a government-sponsored entity. Through OPIC, an American insured can protect its investment, such as a factory or a distributorship, in one of the world's less developed, but developing, nations. OPIC provides insurance against losses of such investments resulting from currency inconvertibility, expropriation, war, revolution or insurrection.

LLOYD'S OF LONDON

Many people think of the legendary Lloyd's of London when the subject of international, or exotic, insurance is mentioned. Actually, Lloyd's is not an insurance company in the ordinary sense of the term, but a marketplace with individual "underwriting members." Its worldwide membership is organized into several hundred syndicates, which in turn may have anywhere from a few to more than 500 participants. Each syndicate is managed by an "underwriter" who accepts or rejects on behalf of the members applications for insurance submitted through brokers.

INDIVIDUAL PARTICIPATION

Lloyd's as a corporation doesn't issue policies, but sets standards with which its members must comply in transacting business with their customers. The policy is prepared by Lloyd's Policy Signing Office, but signed by the individuals who will share any losses.

American insurers' involvement with Lloyd's is primarily as buyers of reinsurance. Also, where a Lloyd's syndicate is the primary insurer of a large risk, it may choose to limit its involvement by reinsuring in the United States.

THE RATEMAKING PROCESS

Where early-day insurers were forced to rely largely on judgment in deciding how much to charge for the coverages they offered, today's highly advanced professionals have the benefit of years of experience upon which to draw in the development of rate structures which reflect varying degrees of risks—or the loss potential—of the many persons or interests they are called upon to insure.

In fire insurance, for example, it is recognized that the likelihood of a "fire-resistive" factory being destroyed by flames is less than the chance of a wooden factory burning down. In automobile insurance, persons who regularly drive their cars to work through rush-hour traffic are exposed to greater hazards than persons who drive only occasionally for pleasure in the same city or community.

RATING FACTORS

For the major lines of property/casualty insurance, the rates vary from state to state and even from community to community depending on the accident record of local motorists, the extent of fire protection available for property owners, the prevalence of crime and other factors. But while many such factors are considered in ratemaking, rates basically are dependent on two primary factors:

CLAIM FREQUENCY, SEVERITY

- the frequency of claims (which generally parallels the frequency of such occurrences as auto accidents, fires and thefts).
- the severity, as measured by the cost, of each claim (which in turn is affected by the costs of goods and services for which insurance pays).

In their periodic review of rates, companies use this "loss experience," supplemented by factors reflecting economic trends, as a guide to the amount they will be required to pay for future claims, to meet the costs of doing business (including taxes) and to realize a profit.

It's a complex process. Insurance can't be priced like most products, since the money people pay for it is intended to help cover the cost of unforeseen future happenings—a fire, for example, or an auto accident, or a burglary. Since premiums are paid in advance, the price must be determined before the actual loss costs are known.

Thus, ratemaking is a task which requires special, highly developed skills and training. The insurance specialist responsible for the ratemaking function, known as an actuary, must be at the same time an analyst, an expert mathematician and a predicter of what is likely to happen in the future. The actuary bases his or her predictions on past experience and available information which can be taken as a reliable indicator of future trends.

ACTUARIAL FUNCTION

For example, insurance industry studies indicate that small cars (compacts and subcompacts) are involved in more accidents, on the average, than larger models and that the frequency of personal injury claims is higher among occupants of the smaller vehicles. This suggests that as long as the popularity of small cars continues, auto insurers face the prospect of a worsening loss experience. The situation could improve, however, if the number of big cars on the highways were to decline significantly.

Another factor that ratemakers must take into account is that in some lines of insurance, such as workers' compensation and liability insurance, losses (or claims) often are paid many years after the premium is calculated and the policy is sold.

In short, the actuary must analyze the experience and the outlook for each line of insurance in terms of claims which already have been paid, outstanding losses—some of which may take several years to settle—and even unreported losses which experience says eventually will find their way into the claims files.

RATEMAKING APPROACHES

There are several categories of ratemaking:

Class Rating

In this most frequently used form of ratemaking, large segments of the population with generally similar expectations of having a loss are grouped into separate classes—or classifications—and assigned separate rates reflecting their average degree of risk. The classification system under which car owners customarily are divided into several categories for rating purposes (see page 16) is a prime example.

RATES/ PREMIUMS

In this connection, it is important that a clear distinction be made between insurance rates and insurance premiums. A premium is the amount a policyholder pays for a policy, while a rate is the pricing factor on which any given unit of the premium is based. For example, a car owner usually pays his or her insurance company a single premium. But the policy probably will include both bodily injury and property damage liability coverages along with such other elements as collision and comprehensive fire and theft coverages. The total premium is based on separate rates for each of those units, in most states taking into account the policyholder's age, sex and marital status. The premium is subject further to any discounts or surcharges which might apply—a driver's education discount, for example, or a surcharge resulting from a poor driving record.

MANUAL RATING

These class rates are published in manuals which are used daily, as a basis for determining the proper price of a policy, by persons involved in selling insurance. For the most part, rating by manual applies to insurance for individuals and small businesses.

Judgment Rating

Some insurance categories—ocean marine in particular—do not lend themselves to class rating because of a lack of similarity among individual risks or a lack of sufficient credible statistics. In such cases, both the acceptability of the applicant for coverage and the rate at which the policy will be written is left to the judgment of the underwriter.

Experience Rating

This involves developing a future rate for an insured by modifying the manual rate to reflect the policyholder's actual experience over a period of several years. A form of experience rating with which many car owners are familiar is the surcharge which some companies add to the auto insurance premium of motorists who are held to be responsible for accidents.

Retrospective Rating

Like experience rating, this is a form of merit rating in that it is used as an incentive to encourage safety. It frequently is applied to liability and workers' compensation premiums for large firms, as well as to commercial automobile, product liability and contractors' liability premiums. Under this procedure, an experience rated premium is adjusted at the end of a policy period in accordance with the insured's actual experience.

RATING ORGANIZATIONS

Accuracy in ratemaking is heavily dependent on the availability of the largest possible body of statistics which collectively make up loss experience. Most companies, the smaller ones in particular, normally do not have enough such data of their own to develop statistically sound rates which they could support as being reasonable and neither too high nor too low.

Therefore, for many years property/casualty insurance companies have supported a number of rating organizations which not only use the combined data of their affiliates to develop rates and rating systems, but provide other related services including the creation of standard insurance policies and policy forms.

NATIONAL ORGANIZATIONS

The largest such organization is the Insurance Services Office (ISO), which operates countrywide and computes rates for most major lines of property and casualty insurance. In most states, ISO files advisory rates which members and subscribers may use as filed or as a basis for "deviations" supported by their own experience. In some cases, ISO files rate changes on behalf of member companies, or provides statistical and actuarial data to companies which want to file their own rates.

Another rating and rate advisory organization for personal and commercial lines of insurance is the American Association of Insurance Services, whose membership is comprised principally of small and medium size companies.

SPECIALTY ORGANIZATIONS

The insurance industry also supports a number of specialized rating organizations. The National Council on Compensation Insurance administers rating plans and systems for workers' compensation insurance in most states (state rating organizations perform similar functions in other states). The Surety Association of America establishes fidelity and surety rates and makes rate filings on behalf of members which authorize it to do so. The Crop-Hail Insurance Actuarial Association is a national rating organization and statistical agency for the fields of crop-hail and rain insurance. The Nuclear Insurance Rating Bureau develops rates for insurance to cover properties of nuclear installations.

The Automobile Insurance Plans Service Office serves as a rating organization and/or statistical agent for the automobile (assigned risk) plans in most states.

STATE RATING BUREAUS

A state counterpart of the national rating organizations is the North Carolina Rate Bureau, of which all insurers which sell automobile, homeowners or workers' compensation insurance in the state must be members. On behalf of its members, the bureau files applications for rate changes applicable to those kinds of insurance, subject to the approval or other action of the insurance department.

State rating bureaus perform special functions in Massachusetts and Texas, where rates for certain kinds of insurance are set by state regulatory agencies. The Massachusetts Automobile Insurance Rating Bureau is a statistical organization whose recommendations are considered by the state insurance department in setting auto insurance rates for use in that state.

In Texas, rates for both automobile and property insurance are set by the State Board of Insurance. The board is guided by recommendations of the Texas Automobile Insurance Service Office (for auto insurance) and the Texas Insurance Advisory Association (for property insurance).

THE UNDERWRITING PROCESS

Underwriting is a cornerstone of the insurance process, but the term underwriting is often used to refer to the insurance business generally. Insurance agents, brokers and other insurance employees often are called underwriters. Actually, an underwriter is an insurance company employee who specializes in deciding whether or not to accept a risk for insurance, determining the conditions of accepting a risk and reviewing the loss experience of an accepted risk to determine if it has been satisfactory.

As the modern insurance system developed in England in the 17th century, shipowners would seek out persons willing to bear part of the financial risk of sea voyages. Typically, the owner would prepare a description of the ship, its cargo, the routes to be followed, the seasons, the ports of call and even the names of officers and crew members. These were then circulated among individuals who would consider bearing the financial risk involved. They would be asked to participate in the venture by assuming a part of the risk. Much of this business was conducted at Lloyd's coffeehouse in London. Persons willing to participate in a particular venture would write their names at the bottom of the descriptive sheet of paper, indicating the percentage of the risk they were willing to assume in return for a fee. From this practice comes the term underwriter.

RISK EVALUATION

Underwriting is a decision-making process. The underwriter must evaluate each application for coverage and decide whether to accept it under specified conditions, or to reject it. A primary function of the underwriting department is to promote the company's growth by proper risk selection to achieve an acceptable balance of good and poor risks properly priced for each line of insurance. It is important for the underwriter to exercise good judgment based on clear understanding of the hazards associated with each kind of coverage.

Some risks that do not meet normal standards can be made acceptable by modifications in the nature of the risk, and insurance companies frequently make recommendations for such changes. The condition of an old building, for example, might be such that certain renovations—possibly including the installation of a sprinkler system—will transform it from an unacceptable to an insurable property.

In making decisions on applications for insurance, the underwriter must gather as much information as possible about the risk and evaluate the potential for loss. An important source of such information is the application itself which varies by line of insurance and which includes pertinent data about the applicant and specifics about the risk to be covered.

Often, the underwriter relies heavily on the recommendation of the agent or broker who accepts the application and submits it to the company. Other sources to which an underwriter can turn if additional information is needed include insurance company inspectors and engineers, private inspection companies which can produce financial and other information about the applicant, state motor vehicle departments and other agencies which maintain centralized files for certain types of risks.

UNDERWRITING CRITERIA

The method of decision-making and the amount of flexibility vary with the insurance company and the type of business being insured. In automobile insurance, the underwriter has specific criteria upon which to base decisions, including the pricing of the policy. These criteria include the make and model of the automobile, the owner's past driving record, and other factors.

In considering an application for insurance on property, the underwriter will want to know about such things as the type of construction of the building, the uses to which it is put, the contents and the availability and quality of fire protection services.

Some types of insurance have relatively few specific criteria, and the underwriter must rely on his or her experience and judgment. In ocean marine insurance, the condition of the ship, the experience and reliability of its officers and crew and the routes to be taken are critical. The cargo also is an important factor affecting the risk. Highly flammable or explosive goods will affect the loss potential. Answers to questions about these and other points affecting the type and degree of risk must be obtained for an underwriter to determine if insurance can be provided, what coverages are appropriate, and at what cost.

CLAIMS PROCEDURES

An insurance claim is a notice from an individual or organization seeking to recover for a loss that may be covered under an insurance policy.

Most property insurance policies require notification in writing "immediately" or "as soon as practicable," after a loss has occurred. Liability policies usually require written notice as soon after an accident as is feasible, and require forwarding of all papers and documents pertaining to the accident as soon as they are received. Notification may be made to the insured's agent or broker, or directly to the insurance company.

LOSS DOCUMENTATION

The insurer will not be liable for any settlement agreement or other arrangement the policyholder may make independently. Only the insurance company's representative can commit the company. If a motorist were to offer a reward for the return of his or her stolen car, for example, the insurer would not be liable for payment of the reward.

The claimant may be required to produce accurate documentation of the loss and estimates for replacement and repairs. Records may be required to assure that claims are valid and fair.

Once the insurance company has determined that a policy is in effect and the loss is covered under the terms of the policy, an adjuster is assigned to verify and determine the amount of loss.

THE ADJUSTER

The adjuster may be an employee of the insurance company or an independent adjuster who handles losses for insurers. Some independent adjusters are highly-trained specialists with wide experience in handling certain types of complicated losses. Losses stemming from grain elevator fires, oil blowouts, mine explosions and similar disasters often require unusual expertise on the part of the adjuster. Public adjusters offer their services to claimants who may want an independent evaluation of a loss.

Most insurance claims are adjusted promptly. Some, however, require prolonged investigation, often because the extent of loss or the cause of loss is unclear. Product liability and professional malpractice claims are among the most difficult to adjust and the most likely to be decided before a judge and jury.

In startling contrast are settlements for claims resulting from destruction caused by natural catastrophes, such as hurricanes and tornadoes. When these disasters strike, adjusters are on the scene within hours and often are able to issue within a day or two partial payment checks to policyholders whose homes have been damaged or destroyed.

ARBITRATION

In attempting to assess the value of damaged property, the insured and insurer sometimes fail to reach an agreement. The amount of the loss in such instances may be arbitrated. The policyholder and the insurance company each designate and pay for the services of an appraiser, and the two appraisers select a third disinterested person to act as referee. The fee of the referee is shared equally by the insured and the insurance company. An amount approved by any two of the arbitrators is binding on both the insured and insurer. Should arbitration fail, the dispute may be resolved in court.

Where there are pending or disputed claims, insurance companies estimate as closely as possible the amounts that will be paid ultimately and set up reserve funds for unpaid losses. However carefully an estimate may be made, it is, nevertheless, subject to a number of uncertainties. A workers' compensation claim, for instance, can result in benefit payments for the duration of disability, which could be an uncertain matter, or payments to a worker's widow for her lifetime.

LOSS SETTLEMENTS

Once the amount of loss has been determined, the insurance company may compensate the insured for property damage by a cash payment or by repairing, rebuilding or replacing. Cash payment is the general practice.

Similarly, with respect to an automobile physical damage claim, the insurance company may repair or replace the automobile or its parts, but again, it usually pays for the loss in cash. It is not liable for more than the value of the car prior to the loss.

As for theft losses, should the stolen property be recovered, the insurance company may return the property to the policyholder and pay for damages that may have occurred as a result of the theft. Or it may retain the property and, in settlement, pay the policyholder the actual cash value.

Settlement with the insured does not always close the books on a claim. If a third party caused the loss, the insurance company may try to recover from that party what it paid to its own policyholder. In the case of a collision, for instance, the insurance company might pay for the damage to its policyholder's car and then seek reimbursement from the car owner who was responsible for the accident, or that person's insurer.

INSURANCE CATASTROPHE PROCEDURES

A catastrophe, in the language of insurers, is an exceptionally severe loss, as from a devastating fire, hurricane or tornado. Man-made catastrophes, such as an oil spill accident, a spacecraft plummeting to earth or an explosion, could cause equally massive losses. Standard insurance coverages protect against loss from these life- and property-threatening occurrences, but these special cases usually demand special responses by insurers.

In the event of a catastrophe, emergency claims procedures assist the insured victims. Trained claims personnel set up on-site operations, and additional adjusters often are flown in from other areas of the country, to expedite claims handling. As a rule of thumb, an event may be designated as a catastrophe when the insured loss is expected to exceed a million dollars. The industry assigns a serial number to each catastrophe and each claim arising from a particular disaster is "red-flagged" with the number so that total losses for each catastrophe can

$1,000,000 CRITERION

be tabulated. While all losses will be adjusted and payments made as quickly as possible, hardship cases generally are handled first.

ADVANCE PAYMENTS

Adjusters often make advance payments on the spot to assist catastrophe victims. Policyholders may be reimbursed, pending a final settlement of their claims, for reasonable immediate expenses, such as for making temporary repairs, for preventing additional damage or for temporary living expenses.

Catastrophic occurrences usually mean catastrophic dollar losses for insurers. In September of 1979, for instance, Hurricane Frederic resulted in estimated insured losses of $752.5 million, at the time a record for any single catastrophe. Ten states and a number of insurers were affected, and the companies serving the area were hit overnight with very large losses.

How did insurers pay the sudden fortunes demanded of them? The first payment source is insurance premiums and a company's policyholders' surplus (see page 122). Insurers make reinsurance agreements with other companies as a backup payment method. Although catastrophe reinsurance agreements differ, most limit the amount the primary insurer will pay—either for a catastrophic loss to a single policyholder or an entire line of insurance—above which the reinsurer accepts the loss. These agreements are an insurer's security measure against insolvency due to a catastrophic loss.

Industry service to policyholders, and to the general public, begins long before a catastrophe occurs. On a continuing basis, loss prevention and safety information is disseminated by insurers and by industry organizations in areas which are particularly vulnerable to such disasters as hurricanes and tornadoes.

INSURANCE ACCOUNTING AND FINANCIAL REPORTING

What happens to the premium dollar paid by a policyholder to a property or casualty insurance company? How do insurance companies make money?

To understand insurance company finances, it must be realized that there are two basic systems of accounting required by law for insurers. The first system, called *statutory accounting,* is designed to monitor insurance companies to assure payment of claims. The second system, *generally accepted accounting principles,* is designed to provide information for investors.

STATUTORY ACCOUNTING

FINANCIAL MONITORING PROCEDURE

The statutory accounting system was devised by regulators to permit effective monitoring of the financial condition of insurance companies. In the 19th century, most property or casualty insurance companies limited their operations to certain geographical locations or to certain lines of insurance. When a catastrophe occurred, some insurance companies providing property coverages in an affected area were bankrupted. The thrust of early state regulation was to protect the policyholder by trying to make sure an insurance company could pay its claims. In order to do so, state regulators and legislators created the conservative statutory accounting system.

Statutory accounting requires companies to place the full

amount of every premium dollar into an unearned premium reserve fund at the beginning of the policy period even though they must pay out "up front" certain expenses, such as sales commissions and premium taxes. These "up front" expenses must be covered with money borrowed from the insurance company's existing capital. This procedure provides the regulator with one means, in the public's interest, of gauging a company's financial ability to pay claims.

"EARNING" THE PREMIUM

The unearned premium reserve is maintained to enable insurers to satisfy their obligation to policyholders who, in the event the policy is cancelled or otherwise terminated, are entitled to receive a refund based on the length of time remaining in the policy period. Therefore, at the approximate rate of one twelfth each month, the amount of an annual premium is "earned" by the company and is used to pay losses, loss adjustment expenses and company operating costs.

To further assure the ability of insurance companies to pay claims, regulators limit the types of investments (admitted assets) that insurers can make.

Property/casualty insurance companies may invest in stocks and bonds, as well as in real estate used to conduct their insurance business. General real estate investments, such as providing mortgages for properties not used as offices by the insurer, are considered admitted assets up to a limit. The purpose of this requirement is to have property/casualty insurance funds in investments that can readily be sold so that payment of claims in the event of a catastrophe is assured.

On the other hand, life insurance companies, because their claims payouts are more precisely predictable, invest a sizeable amount of their assets in real estate.

GENERALLY ACCEPTED ACCOUNTING PRINCIPLES

SEC REQUIREMENT

The other basic accounting system used by insurers is called the *Generally Accepted Accounting Principles* (GAAP) method. Required by the Securities and Exchange Commission for companies with publicly traded securities, this system was developed to provide financial information to keep persons informed in making their investment decisions. The GAAP System allows insurers to amortize costs such as agent commissions and premium taxes over the period to which the income generated by these expenses applies. GAAP differs in other ways from the statutory accounting method, such as allowing companies to anticipate income from the salvage of properties on which they have paid claims.

CASH FLOW

The diagram on page 125 shows what happens to the premium dollar paid to a property/casualty insurance company. In simplified terms, the diagram traces the distribution of the premium dollar from the time it is paid by the policyholder. It also shows the underwriting and the investment aspects of a company's operation.

POLICYHOLDERS' SURPLUS

The key to an insurer's financial health is the state of its "policyholders' surplus" account. For capital stock insurers, policyholders' surplus consists of retained earnings as well as capital paid in by stockholders. In the case of mutual and reciprocal companies, it consists of amounts paid by policyholders and others to create a surplus to meet licensing requirements. It is the net worth of the company after subtraction of all liabilities from all assets. This account serves as an extra backup to a company's reserves so that money will be available to pay catastrophic or unexpectedly severe losses. Also, the policyholders' surplus is the account into which future retained earnings will be placed in order to increase the company's financial base to provide capital for additional insurance demanded by a growing society. Thus, the term "surplus" refers not to excess or unneeded funds, but to the funds required to guarantee insurance company solvency.

UNEARNED PREMIUM RESERVE

The full amount of the premium paid by a policyholder is placed into the company's unearned premium reserve until it is "earned" during the policy period. The company earns a premium as time elapses during the policy term, i.e., after six months on a one-year policy, the company has "earned" one-half of the premium. The portion of the premium withheld as commission by the agent is borrowed from policyholders' surplus to meet the statutory accounting requirement. The premium becomes fully earned by the company upon the termination of the policy period.

The diagram on page 125 illustrates how the company pays claims and creates loss reserves to pay unsettled claims. It also shows expenditures for other business operations including taxes and fees. If there is a balance, the company records a statutory underwriting profit. If there is a deficit, the company records a statutory underwriting loss. Policyholder dividends are paid by some companies from underwriting profit, or under

UNDERWRITING PROFIT/LOSS

certain kinds of rating plans such as retrospective rating plans for workers' compensation. Since policyholder dividends are a refund of premiums earned, they represent a reduction of income. An insurance company's overall underwriting results are calculated by subtracting policyholder dividends from the company's statutory underwriting profit or adding them to the company's statutory underwriting loss.

INVESTMENT INCOME

Total investment income is derived from the investment of unearned premium reserves, loss reserves and the policyholders' surplus. After deducting investment expenses from the investment income, the insurance company can calculate its net investment gain. This figure, together with the underwriting profit or loss (after any dividends to policyholders), is the company's net operating income or loss for the year. Investment income generally reflects interest, rents, dividends on stocks and capital gains or losses realized from the sales of stocks and bonds. Unrealized capital gains or losses, such as a decline or gain in stock value of the insurer's investment holdings which are not sold, are reflected in the changed financial worth of the policyholders' surplus account. The value of bonds held by insurance companies in the policyholders' surplus account is calculated at their amortized value, rather than at the prevailing market value, on the assumption that bonds are held to maturity, at which time the full value of the bond is recoverable. If there is net income, it is added to policyholders' surplus to support future growth. In the case of capital stock companies, a portion of the net income may be used to pay dividends to stockholders.

RATIOS

Often, financial analysts and others will discuss various ratios applicable to the operation of the insurance business. Among these ratios is the *loss ratio,* which is determined by dividing the losses incurred (both paid losses and amounts set aside to pay future losses) and loss adjustment expenses by the premiums earned. Premiums earned are used since claim losses cannot occur on unearned premiums. The *expense ratio* is determined by dividing underwriting expenses (company overhead costs and costs involved in the sales process, such as commissions) by the premiums written. Premiums written are used because they are directly related to the operating (overhead) and acquisition (sales) costs.

To obtain a rough measure of a company's or the industry's

COMBINED RATIO

profitability, the loss ratio and the expense ratio are added to create the *combined ratio*. If the combined ratio is more than 100, it indicates that the insurer had a statutory underwriting loss. Combined ratios under 100 indicate a statutory underwriting profit. This profitability measure is only approximate since it utilizes ratios with two different bases (premium earned and premium written).

Other tests such as the ratio of premiums written to policyholders' surplus, as well as the ratio of loss reserves to policyholders' surplus, are used as guidelines by regulators and financial analysts to evaluate financial solidity of insurers.

Traditionally, some insurance business observers have advocated a 2-to-1 premium to surplus ratio ($2 of premium for each $1 of surplus), but agree that the ratio will vary by the type of insurance sold by a company.

TAXES

Insurance companies pay taxes in three basic categories: state premium taxes, local taxes/fees and federal and state income tax.

STATE PREMIUM TAXES

State premium taxes, averaging about 2 per cent, are levied against the gross receipts (premiums written) of an insurer, regardless of overall profit or loss. Premium taxes paid to the 50 states by property/casualty insurance companies totaled more than $1.5 billion in 1980. Insurers also pay real estate taxes, and various use taxes, as well as state license fees. Federal income taxes are based on profit from underwriting and/or investment income.

To calculate income and profit or loss for federal tax purposes, Congress passed laws generally accepting the statutory accounting method required by state regulators, with some modifications.

PROFITABILITY

A company's bottom line operating gain or loss is made up of its underwriting results together with its investment results. State regulators traditionally have allowed an underwriting profit margin in setting rates. However, the property/casualty insurance business is highly cyclical, with underwriting results fluctuating from periods of profit to periods of loss. Investment income is derived from the sale of equities, as well as from interest and dividends. Unrealized capital gains or losses, i.e., when the market value of stocks rise or fall but the securities

CASH FLOW DIAGRAM

PROPERTY/CASUALTY INSURANCE COMPANIES

(A simplified model)

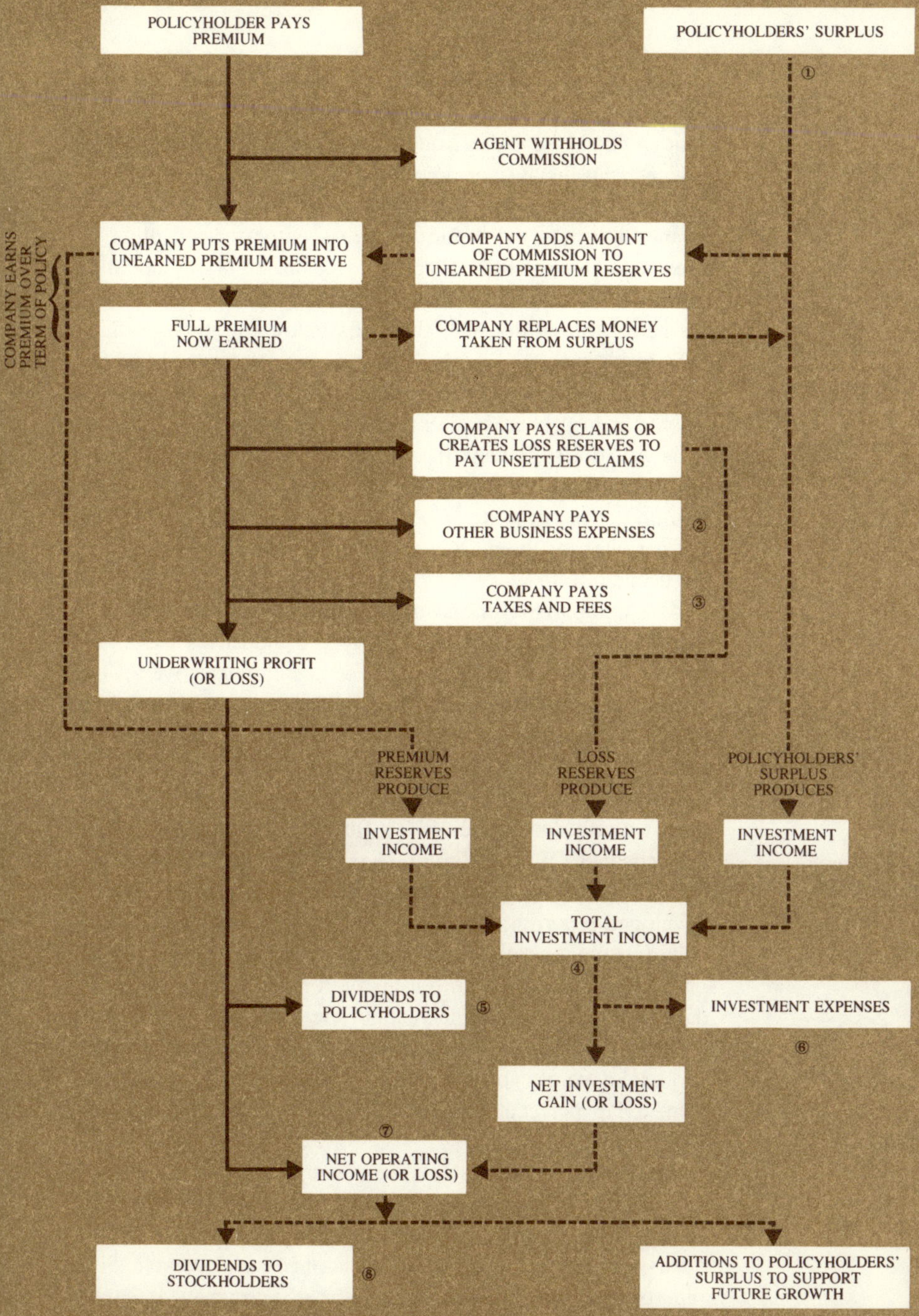

① The excess of assets over liabilities
② Overhead costs—rent, salaries, etc
③ Federal, state and local taxes, licenses and fees. Actually, insurers pay these taxes at various stages
④ Includes interest, dividends, rents and realized capital gains
⑤ On certain lines only
⑥ Costs of operating the company's investment program
⑦ If underwriting loss exceeds investment gain, there will be a net operating loss
⑧ Applies only in the case of capital stock companies

are not sold, are not reflected in investment income. However, unrealized capital changes on securities do affect an insurer's policyholders' surplus. Bond values are reflected in policyholders' surplus at their amortized, not market, value.

In the decades since the 1940's, the property/casualty insurance business in certain years has outperformed other financial industries in profitability. But the highly competitive nature of the business with about 2,900 companies generally has held profitability over the years below the average of all U.S. industries.

MEASURES OF PROFITABILITY

One measure of profitability is the annual rate of return (net income from all sources after taxes) on net worth. Data collected by New York's Citibank (see table, page 127) show that property/casualty insurance companies' average annual rate of return on net worth was 5.7 per cent for the decade of 1950-59; 4.2 per cent for the decade of 1960-69, and 12.1 per cent for the decade of 1970-79.

As a comparison, the average annual rates of return on net worth for the same time periods for all industries were 10.9 per cent, 9.9 per cent and 12.3 per cent, respectively. The average annual rates of return on net worth for the same time periods for utilities were 9.5 per cent, 10.5 per cent and 11.1 per cent.

Illustrating the cyclical nature of insurance, the rate of return on net worth during the 1970's fluctuated from a low of 1.5 per cent in 1975 to a high of 21.0 per cent in 1977.

The National Association of Insurance Commissioners (NAIC) developed reporting systems in 1971 to measure property/casualty insurance profitability in a variety of ways, including not only return on net worth but also return on sales. The NAIC data covering the last nine years of the 1970's showed that the industry's annual operating profit or loss (after income taxes and exclusive of capital gains) as a percentage of sales ranged from a 1.8 per cent loss in 1975 to a 5.9 per cent profit in 1978.

NAIC's reporting systems were designed to aid state insurance regulators in evaluating whether competition is effective in regulating prices and whether insurance company and industry profits are sufficient to attract necessary capital. Such reports also may indicate if an insurance company is having financial difficulties.

The combined system of statutory accounting and generally

AVERAGE ANNUAL RATES OF RETURN—NET INCOME AFTER TAXES—AS A PER CENT OF NET WORTH OF SELECTED INDUSTRIES (a)

Year	Property & Casualty Insurance	Manu-facturing	Public Utilities	Services	Commercial Banks	All Industries
1950	8.0	17.1	9.8	10.5	8.3	13.3
1951	5.7	14.4	9.0	9.8	7.6	11.4
1952	7.3	12.3	9.0	9.6	7.9	10.3
1953	7.0	12.5	9.2	11.0	7.8	10.5
1954	7.0	12.4	9.3	11.8	9.3	10.3
1955	5.5	15.0	9.7	12.3	7.9	12.0
1956	2.2	13.9	9.8	13.2	7.7	11.3
1957	1.8	12.8	9.6	12.7	8.3	10.6
1958	5.6	9.8	9.8	9.9	9.7	9.0
1959	6.8	11.6	10.1	10.4	7.9	9.8
Average Annual Rate (1950-59)	5.7	13.2	9.5	11.1	8.2	10.9
1960	5.9	10.6	9.9	9.1	10.1	9.1
1961	4.4	9.9	9.9	10.4	9.6	8.5
1962	4.2	10.9	10.0	10.9	8.9	8.9
1963	3.1	11.6	10.2	10.5	9.0	9.4
1964	2.5	12.6	10.7	11.8	8.8	10.0
1965	2.2	13.9	10.8	14.4	8.7	10.8
1966	5.5	14.2	11.0	16.2	8.6	11.0
1967	5.5	12.6	11.0	15.9	9.6	10.5
1968	4.7	13.3	10.6	16.3	9.4	10.5
1969	3.7	12.4	10.8	13.4	10.1	10.0
Average Annual Rate (1960-69)	4.2	12.2	10.5	12.9	9.3	9.9
1970	9.1	10.1	10.5	10.1	10.4	9.1
1971	13.2	10.8	10.3	11.1	10.6	10.2
1972	12.9	12.1	10.3	12.1	10.5	10.6
1973	9.5	14.9	10.6	12.9	12.6	11.9
1974	5.2	15.2	10.4	13.5	10.7	12.3
1975	1.5	12.6	11.0	15.0	10.3	11.1
1976	10.8	15.0	11.5	18.1	12.2	13.2
1977	21.0	14.9	12.1	18.3	13.0	13.7
1978	20.9	15.9	12.1	21.2	14.7	14.7
1979	17.2	18.4	12.3	19.9	15.6	16.3
Average Annual Rate (1970-79)	12.1	14.0	11.1	15.2	12.1	12.3

a) Net worth at the beginning of each year; equivalent to "book net assets" or stockholders' equity.

Source: *Corporate Profits Tabulations*—Economics Department—CITIBANK.

accepted accounting principles, together with the special gauges of profitability created by the NAIC, have helped to assure the continuing ability of the property/casualty insurance business to meet fully the needs and demands of the nation's insuring public.

REGULATION

As a business whose primary function is to protect the financial stability of its customers, property and casualty insurance long has been subject to close regulation by designated authorities in every state, the District of Columbia, American Samoa, Guam, Puerto Rico and the Virgin Islands.

Because the industry has a high degree of competition, the desirability of certain safeguards embodied in the state regulatory system is well recognized as being consistent with the public interest.

SOLVENCY SAFEGUARDS

History suggests that the basic charge to which the regulators are committed is essentially the same as what New Hampshire lawmakers had in mind when they established the nation's first structured regulatory body back in 1851. The state mandated that one member of a three-member insurance board make at least once a year "a full examination into the condition of each company and the management of its affairs."

FUNCTIONS OF REGULATORS

Today's procedures are much more complex, but the monitoring of insurance companies' financial condition continues to be a primary responsibility of regulators, to assure that the companies remain solvent and thus able to meet their obligations to policyholders.

Where companies encounter financial hardships in spite of this careful oversight, the state regulators are empowered to take steps to protect the public's interest, including liquidation if necessary. A faltering company may be placed in the hands of a rehabilitator in an effort to restore it to a sound operating position.

To protect insurance claimants against the adverse effects which could result from company insolvencies, every state has established a procedure under which solvent companies absorb the losses of the insolvent insurers. New York maintains a permanent insolvency fund, while the other states have established insurance guaranty associations through which solvent insurers pay assessments, as required, on a proportionate basis to insure payments to persons who have claims against an insolvent company.

GUARANTY FUNDS

While their powers vary from state to state, the regulatory officials generally are charged with licensing and monitoring insurance companies, approving the form and conditions of policies and reviewing rate changes to ascertain that customers are not overcharged or unfairly discriminated against and that rate levels are adequate to maintain a company's solvency.

RATING LAWS

The procedures for reviewing and putting into effect the rates on which policyholders' premiums are based are reflected in state rating laws which provide varying degrees of flexibility. There are several types of rating laws:

PRIOR APPROVAL

- Prior approval laws, under which companies must file statistically-supported applications for rate changes, which then must be approved by the state regulator before they may be put into effect. Some of these laws have "deemer" provisions under which rates are deemed to have been approved if the regulator has taken no action within a specified period.
- Competitive rating laws, which permit companies to make rate changes as needed, subject to the constraining forces of the competitive marketplace. In turn, the competitive rating statutes take a number of forms:

COMPETITIVE RATING

Open competition laws, under which companies are allowed to adjust rates without going through the formality of filing a notice with the regulatory agency. In states which have such laws, however, rates are subject to monitoring by the insurance regulator who can take appropriate action if the rates are found to be excessive, inadequate or unfairly discriminatory.

File and use laws, which require companies to file notice of rate changes but permit the use of the new rates upon filing and until or unless the regulator subsequently disapproves them.

Use and file laws, a variation of file and use under which companies may put rate changes into effect and later submit an informational filing which becomes subject to regulatory review.

Rate revisions may be filed either by individual companies or by rating organizations on behalf of groups of companies.

EVOLUTION OF STATE REGULATORY LAWS

While property and casualty insurance, like any other component of the private enterprise system in the United States, is subject to certain kinds of federal regulatory controls (such as statutes governing taxes and fair employment practices), the primary regulation of the business has been the concern of the individual states since New Hampshire created its three-member examining board in 1851.

NAIC

Several other states followed New Hampshire's lead in the 1850's and 1860's, and 19 states were represented in 1871 at the organizational meeting of the National Insurance Convention, the forerunner of today's National Association of Insurance Commissioners (NAIC). The NAIC, of which all state regulators are members, has among its main goals the promotion of uniformity in state supervision of insurance matters and the development of model insurance legislation.

Three major developments have marked the history of insurance regulation in the United States. Following aborted efforts in the late 1860's to create a federal bureau of insurance, the Supreme Court ruled in 1869 (in *Paul v. Virginia*) that issuing an insurance policy was not a transaction of commerce and thus was not subject to the interstate commerce clause of the Constitution.

SEUA DECISION

That decision clearly left regulation of the business to the states, and was not successfully challenged until 1944. At that time, the Supreme Court was asked to rule on a charge that the South-Eastern Underwriters Association (SEUA), a rating organization, was in violation of the Sherman Anti-Trust Act by conspiring to fix and maintain arbitrary and non-competitive fire insurance rates and by conspiring to monopolize trade and commerce in fire insurance in six southern states. The court in effect reversed its earlier decision, declaring insurance to be interstate commerce and thus subject to federal anti-trust laws.

The SEUA decision opened the door to federal regulation, but did not effectively rule out state regulation. The next step was left to the Congress.

McCARRAN-FERGUSON ACT

Congress was quick to rectify the situation with the passage in 1945 of the McCarran-Ferguson Act (Public Law 15). The McCarran-Ferguson Act provided that effective in 1948 federal fair trade and anti-trust laws would apply to the insurance business only "to the extent that such business is not regulated by state law," except in cases of boycott, coercion and intimidation, which remained under federal control.

Given the 1948 deadline, the states had three years to demonstrate, through amendments to existing laws or enactment of new statutes, that they could properly supervise the insurance business. An all-industry committee sponsored by the National Association of Insurance Commissioners was charged with the development of a "model" law which would fill the need.

ALL-INDUSTRY COMMITTEE

The regulatory approach embodied in the resulting model law embraced the concept of "prior approval" of rates. Insurers would be permitted to make rates in concert through membership in rating organizations, but could not put them into effect until they had been submitted to and approved by the state regulatory authorities.

Most of the states adopted that approach. Several others enacted "file and use" statutes with only one—California—opting at that time for an "open competition" rating law.

Over the succeeding quarter-century, the environment in which insurers operate changed dramatically from one in which many companies used the same rates and forms to one characterized by a high intensity of competition, with different rates and forms being used. Major factors which contributed to the change were:

- the development in the 1950's of multiple-line packages for both home owners and businesses and the resulting growth of "multiple-line" insurance companies.
- the rise to competitive prominence of "direct writers"—companies which market insurance through their own exclusive agents. (In the late 1940's, the property/casualty insurance business had been dominated by companies which specialized either in property insurance or in cas-

ualty insurance, and which merchandised their products through independent local agents and brokers.)

- entry into the property/casualty insurance field of several of the nation's largest life insurance companies.

TREND TOWARD REGULATED COMPETITION

The late 1960's saw the beginning of a significant trend—which has continued through the seventies and into the eighties—toward greater reliance on the forces of the competitive marketplace as being in the best interests of the public as well as of state regulators and the property/casualty insurance business itself. A number of states replaced their prior approval regulatory laws with statutes providing for forms of competitive ratemaking, based on the philosophy that:

- reliance on price competition in the marketplace tends to produce the most equitable rates;
- regulators are freed from the time-consuming task of reviewing thousands of rate filings—often on a tight timetable—and are able to devote greater attention and resources to surveying insurance company solvency and consumer-related matters.
- market freedom generates product and marketing innovations which heighten competition, promote improvements in products and services and increase insurer responsiveness to changing consumer needs and desires.

MIX OF RATING LAWS

By 1980, varying forms of competitive rating laws were operative in 22 states in which about half of the nation's property and casualty insurance is written. In some states, rates are subject to prior approval for some kinds of property and casualty insurance but are competitively established for others.

In Texas, rates for automobile and property insurance are set by the State Board of Insurance, which is guided by recommendations of two industry-supported rating bureaus. In Massachusetts, a rating bureau recommends, but the state insurance department sets, rates for private passenger automobile insurance.

In 1980, Illinois was the only state without a rating law. However, another Illinois law expressly prohibits insurance companies from agreeing with each other or with an advisory (rating) organization to adhere to the use of statistics, policies or underwriting rules. Thus, the environment in which insurers operate in that state is among the nation's most competitive.

In December, 1980, the National Association of Insurance

Commissioners (NAIC) approved a Model Competitive Pricing Law, embracing the philosophy that the cost of insurance within a state should be determined more by competition among insurers than by state rate regulation. In drafting the model law, the NAIC was aided by a 23-member advisory committee comprising a cross section of insurance company executives, insurance agents, representatives of rating organizations, consumer groups and scholars. After a year's deliberations, the advisory committee issued a 202-page report supporting the general conclusion "that price competition, where properly structured and free of unnecessary impediments, is the most effective way to assure the availability of property/casualty insurance at costs that are fair, reasonable and not excessive."

MODEL PRICING LAW

LOSS PREVENTION

"An ounce of prevention is worth a pound of cure," said Benjamin Franklin, who ought to know, since he was a founder of Philadelphia's first volunteer fire brigade, The Union Fire Company as well as the country's first successful fire insurance company, the Philadelphia Contributionship for the Insurance of Houses from Loss by Fire. Immediately after launching the Contributionship (1752), Franklin also started a clean-up campaign which taught Philadelphians how to recognize and remove fire hazards from their homes and grounds. He developed the lightning rod as an anti-fire measure, and the still-popular Franklin stove was designed to provide more heat than an open fire, while containing the potentially dangerous blaze.

FRANKLIN'S INFLUENCE

Loss prevention and insurance have gone hand-in-hand ever since. Insurance companies, agencies and brokerage firms provide safety inspection and engineering services to commercial and industrial clients as part and parcel of their service. Indeed, they often require their clients to meet certain safety standards before obtaining insurance, and help them to do so.

Many industries, taking the lead from insurers, apply loss prevention techniques to their operations on their own. Risk managers, industrial hygienists, loss control engineers, and inspectors are common additions to modern industrial staffs. Their professional training enables them to identify and prevent different types of losses or to correct the causes after losses occur.

ORGANIZATIONS

The insurance industry has formed, funded or contributed to many organizations devoted to reducing accidents, injuries or other losses. The functions of these organizations range from safety and training programs to research, testing and engineering studies, and include such activities as anti-crime endeavors and natural disaster emergency plans. Similar activities are carried out both by individual companies and by industry organizations.

TESTING LABORATORIES

An example of such an organization is Underwriters' Laboratories, which is well-known to the public although its relation to the insurance industry may not be so generally known. The UL, whose initials now form a universally recognized safety seal, dates back to 1893, the year of Chicago's Columbian Exposition. After a rash of fires broke out in the exposition, a group of insurance companies hired an expert to find out the reason. Discovering that electrical problems caused the fires, he suggested remedies. The insurers decided to retain him to conduct continuing research into electricity-related fires, and provided facilities that became known as Underwriters' Laboratories. Long operated under insurance industry sponsorship, but now independent, UL today is one of several organizations that test electrical materials and other products to determine that the items meet safety standards.

Other testing laboratories, including some operated by individual insurance companies, have been established in recent years.

Loss prevention is a hallmark of the Industrial Risk Insurers, a "pool" of insurance companies which offers insurance coverage and specializes in advisory fire protection services for highly protected risks—those which require a high degree of loss control—such as oil, chemical and petrochemical plants. It provides engineering, research and hazard testing services, publishes recommended safety practices and maintains a full-time training laboratory.

The Factory Mutual System, a "pool" of insurance companies specializing in insurance of highly protected properties, also places heavy emphasis on hazard control and loss prevention services. The Factory Mutual System conducts loss control inspections and training programs, engineering and research services for its member companies and for industry at large.

Included in the engineering and research services is a network of testing laboratories which conduct basic and applied research for industry loss control apparatus and property conservation including firefighting equipment. As an outgrowth of this, the Factory Mutual System publishes engineering standards for the manufacture of loss control equipment.

ACCIDENT AND CRIME FIGHTERS

Insurance companies fund organizations such as the Insurance Crime Prevention Institute and the National Automobile Theft Bureau to combat fraud and theft, and the Insurance Institute for Highway Safety to reduce motor vehicle accidents and deaths. The industry-wide Insurance Committee for Arson Control is active throughout the country. Working with consumers, local governments, and criminal justice agencies to counter a problem that has become almost epidemic in many communities, it develops awareness of and solutions to the arson problem.

COMMUNICATIONS ACTIVITIES

Insurers and industry-sponsored organizations including the Insurance Information Institute also disseminate information directly to the public and through the news media to areas particularly prone to natural disasters such as hurricanes, tornadoes and even volcanic erruptions. These communications are aimed at educating the public about how to prepare for such catastrophes, what to do when they happen and how to seek help afterwards.

Insurers contribute to the National Crime Prevention Association, the National Fire Protection Association, and the National Safety Council to assist those non-profit organizations to do their vital work.

With industry support, these groups and others work vigorously in such areas as:

- fire protection—building design reviews; fire suppression system evaluations; fire protection plan development;

- occupational safety and health—plant safety inspections; surveys to discover violations before federal agents visit plants or businesses; consultation and advice on OSHA standards; measurement of toxic substances; noise surveys; air sampling and evaluation;
- compliance with boiler and machinery laws and standards;
- burglary protection surveys; crime and loss analysis; security system evaluations;
- products—safety tests; quality control; recall systems;
- highway safety—accident loss analysis; studies of the driving environment, and driver training and testing programs.

LOSS PREVENTION INCENTIVES

Insurers work to raise the consciousness of business people in maintaining a safe environment and in producing safe products, just as they also encourage consumers to use in a safe manner the products they buy.

One method insurers use to encourage workplace safety is "retrospective rating." Under this kind of rating plan, workers' compensation premiums are adjusted upward or downward at the end of the year in accordance with a firm's actual work accident experience. This procedure provides employers with a strong economic incentive to maintain safe working conditions and thereby hold on-the-job accidents to a minimum.

Because worker injury can't be eradicated, insurers employ and support physical and vocational rehabilitation programs to restore disabled workers to gainful employment. Insurers help develop prosthetic devices (artificial body parts), engage in ergonomic research (the study of physical capabilities and the modification of tools and work situations to meet those capabilities), and work closely with employers in an effort to place rehabilitated workers in productive jobs as soon as possible after recovery from a disabling injury or illness.

The consumers' role in preventing losses should not be overlooked. The insurance industry contributes to public education campaigns supporting safe driving at recommended speeds in well-maintained vehicles, stressing the benefits of home smoke detection and security systems, and promoting other forms of safety awareness ashore and afloat.

CONSUMER AWARENESS

MAKING THE BEST USE OF INSURANCE

Despite the effectiveness of loss prevention programs, accidents and other losses are bound to happen. Most people buy insurance as a safeguard against such losses, but the purchase of insurance is not an end in itself.

Invariably, consumers will have questions—where and how to shop for insurance, what kinds of protection are afforded by their policies, and what to do if they have an insurance-related problem.

The first step is to find the right agent, broker or company representative, perhaps by consulting a friend or neighbor—or even the telephone book. Agents and brokers are able to answer any questions about the insurance policies they sell, and they serve in a liaison capacity between the insurance company and the consumer.

Most state insurance departments have personnel whose responsibilities include working directly with consumers who have complaints or differences of opinion with their insurers.

For consumers to make the best use of insurance, they should have a clear understanding of what is available to them, the coverages included in their policies, and what to do in the event of a loss. This book is intended to help bring about a better understanding of property/casualty insurance.

APPENDIX

GLOSSARY OF INSURANCE TERMS

Acquisition Cost: The cost to an insurer of securing business, such as advertising, sales promotions and agent's and broker's commissions.

Actual Cash Value: The cost of repairing or replacing damaged property with property of the same kind and quality and in the same physical condition; commonly defined as replacement cost less depreciation.

Actuary: An insurance professional whose primary functions include the determination of rates and rating methods, evaluation of reserves and other statistic-related responsibilities.

Additional Living Expense: The extra, above-normal, costs of such expenses as food and lodging incurred while a home damaged by an insured peril is being repaired. These additional costs are covered in all forms of the homeowners policy.

Adjuster: A person who seeks to determine the amount of loss suffered when an insurance claim is submitted and attempts to settle the claim.

Admitted Company: An insurance company licensed and authorized to do business in a particular state.

Agent: The **independent agent** is an independent businessman who usually represents two or more insurance companies under contract in a sales and service capacity and who is paid on a commission basis. The **exclusive agent** represents only one company, usually on a commission basis. The **direct writer** is the salaried or commissioned employee of a single company.

Alien Insurance Company: An insurance company incorporated under the laws of a foreign country.

Allied Lines: A term for forms of insurance allied with fire insurance, covering such perils as sprinkler leakage, water damage and earthquake.

All-Risk Policy: A policy covering loss of or damage to property resulting from any peril except those which are specifically excluded.

Appeal Bond: One filed in court by a party against whom a judgment has been rendered, in order to stay execution of the judgment pending appeal to a higher court, in the hope of reversing the judgment. The bond guarantees that the judgment will be paid if the appeal fails.

Apportionment: The dividing of a loss proportionately among two or more insurers which cover the same loss.

Appraisal: A survey to determine a property's insurable value or the amount of a loss.

Appurtentant Structures: Buildings on the same premises as the main building insured under a property insurance policy.

Arbitration: A binding procedure to settle a dispute between an insurance company and an insured over a claim settlement by placing the decision in the hands of an appraiser appointed by each party to the dispute and a third disinterested person by the two appraisers.

Arson: The willful and malicious burning of, or attempt to burn, any structure or other property, often with criminal or fraudulent intent.

Assessment: The extra premium a mutual or reciprocal insurer's policyholder may be required to pay in the event the insurer's losses are greater than anticipated.

Assets: As applicable to insurance, all funds, property, goods, securities, rights of action or resources of any kind owned by an insurance company, less such items as are declared non-admissible by state laws, including deferred or overdue premiums.

Assigned Risk Plan: See Automobile Insurance Plan.

Assurance: A term synonymous to insurance, although used more frequently when referring to life insurance.

Automobile Insurance Plan: Formerly called and still sometimes referred to as "assigned risk" plan. A program to make automobile insurance available to persons who are unable to obtain such insurance in the voluntary market.

Automobile Liability Insurance: Protection for the insured against financial loss because of legal liability for car-related injuries to others or damage to their property.

Automobile Physical Damage Insurance: Coverage for damages or loss to the policyholder's automobile, resulting from collision, fire, theft and other perils.

Average Adjuster: An individual specializing in ocean marine losses involving general average. (See General Average).

Aviation Insurance: Insurance pertaining to aircraft, including coverage of aircraft or their contents, the owner's liability or accident insurance on the passengers.

Bail Bond: A bond which guarantees the appearance of a person in court, and which is subject to forfeiture if that person violates the provisions of the bond.

Bailee: One who has temporary possession of property belonging to another.

Basic Form: A package insurance policy providing coverage against a limited number of specified perils.

Blanket Coverage: Insurance covering more than one item of property at a single location or two or more items of property in different locations.

Block Policy: An all-risk inland marine policy covering all property on or off a merchant's premises, including property of others in the care, custody or control of the policyholder.

Bodily Injury Liability Insurance: Protection against loss arising out of the liability imposed upon the policyholder by law for damages because of bodily injury, sickness, disease or death suffered by another person or persons.

Boiler and Machinery Insurance: Coverage for loss arising out of the operation of pressure, mechanical and electrical equipment. It may cover loss to the boiler and machinery itself, damage to other property, and business interruption losses.

Bond: Generally speaking, an agreement whereby one party, called the surety, obligates itself to a second party, called the obligee, to answer for the default of a third party, called the principal.

Broad Form: A package policy providing coverage for the same perils covered in the basic form, plus specified additional perils.

Broker: A marketing specialist who represents buyers of property and liability insurance and who deals with either agents or companies in arranging for the coverage required by the customer.

Burglary: Breaking and entering into another person's property with felonious intent.

Burglary and Theft Insurance: Protection for loss of property due to burglary, robbery or larceny.

Business Interruption Insurance: Protection for a business owner against losses resulting from a temporary shutdown because of fire or other insured peril. The insurance provides reimbursement for lost net profits and necessary continuing expenses.

Buy-Out Policy: A professional liability policy covering future claims resulting from incidents which occurred during the period that an expired claims-made policy was in force.

Cancellation: Termination of an insurance policy or bond by an insurance company or a policyholder before its expiration date.

Capacity: A measure of the amount of insurance which an insurance company is able or prepared to assume on particular risks.

Capital Stock Insurance Company: An insurance company which is owned and controlled by stockholders, or investors.

Captive Insurer: An insurance company set up by a company or groups of companies to insure their own risks or risks common to the group.

Cargo Insurance: Insurance covering goods being transported by some conveyance such as a ship, train or truck.

Casualty Insurance: Insurance concerned primarily with the insured's legal liability for injuries to others or for damage to other persons' property; also encompasses such forms of insurance as plate glass, burglary, robbery and aviation.

Catastrophe: In insurance, a term applied for statistical recording purposes to an incident or a series of related incidents involving an insured loss expected to exceed a million dollars.

Cede: To buy or effect reinsurance. The transfer of all or a part of one insurer's liability to a reinsurer.

Cession: A yielding of a property or right under a reinsurance agreement.

Claim: A demand to recover under an insurance policy for a loss covered by that policy.

Claims-Made Form: A type of liability policy which covers claims which occur and are reported while the policy is in effect.

Classification: The grouping, for underwriting, rating or other purposes, of policyholders or properties having the same general characteristics.

Coinsurance: A provision in an insurance policy under which the insured, for a reduced rate, agrees to carry a certain amount of insurance expressed as a percentage of the value of his or her property. It provides for the full payment, up to the amount of the policy, of all losses if the insurance carried is at least equal to the specified percentage. However, if the insured fails to carry the necessary amount of insurance, he or she assumes a proportionate share of the loss.

Collision Insurance: An automobile insurance coverage against damage to the policyholder's vehicle caused by collision with another car or object or by upset.

Combined Ratio: The sum of the ratio of losses incurred to premiums earned and the ratio of commissions and expenses incurred to premiums written.

Commercial Blanket Bond: A fidelity bond to cover operators of commercial establishments against losses resulting from employees' dishonest acts.

Commercial Lines: Insurance for businesses, organizations, institutions, governmental agencies or other commercial establishments.

Commercial Multiple Peril Insurance: A package type of insurance which includes a wide range of essential coverages for the commercial establishment.

Commission: A percentage of an insurance premium paid to an agent or broker for producing and servicing the business.

Commissioner: A state officer responsible for administering the state's insurance laws and regulations. In some states, the regulator bears the title of director or superintendent of insurance.

Competitive State Fund: A facility established by a state to write workers' compensation insurance in competition with private insurers.

Comprehensive Automobile Insurance: Coverage against loss of or damage to a car from a number of perils including fire, theft, windstorm, flood and vandalism (but not including collision or upset).

Comprehensive Insurance: A term used for a variety of policies providing broad protection.

Comprehensive Personal Liability Insurance: Protection for an insured against loss arising out of the policyholder's legal liability to pay money for damage or injury to others. Does not include automobile liability or business operations.

Compulsory Insurance: Any form of insurance which is required by law.

Concealment: The failure to disclose a material fact.

Consequential Loss: A loss resulting from, but not caused directly by, an insured peril. For example, if a fire should damage refrigeration equipment, any spoilage of its contents resulting from the loss of refrigeration would be a consequential loss.

Conditions: Provisions of an insurance policy which state the rights and duties of the insured and the insurer.

Contingent Liability: The liability of individuals, corporations or partnerships for accidents caused by persons other than employees, for whose acts or omissions the individuals, corporations or partnerships are legally responsible.

Contract Bond: A guarantee of the faithful performance of a construction contract and usually the payment of all labor and material bills related to it.

Contractual Liability Insurance: Coverage for a loss for which the policyholder has assumed another's liability under contract.

Countersignature: The signature of a licensed agent or representative on a policy or bond, required by some state laws to validate the contract.

Coverage: The scope of the protection provided under a contract of insurance; any of several risks covered by a policy.

Credit Insurance: A guarantee to manufacturers, wholesalers and service organizations that they will be paid for goods shipped or services rendered. It is a guarantee of that part of their working capital represented by accounts receivable.

Crop-Hail Insurance: Protection against damage to growing crops as a result of hail or certain other named perils.

Declaration: The part of a property or liability insurance policy which includes such information as the name and address of the insured, the property insured, its location and description, the policy period, the amount of insurance coverage, applicable premiums, and supplemental information provided by the insured.

Deductible: An amount which a policyholder agrees to pay, per claim or per accident, toward the total amount of an insured loss. Insurance is written on this basis at reduced rates.

Depreciation: A decrease in the value of property due to wear and tear or obsolescence.

Direct Writer: An insurer whose distribution mechanism is either the direct selling system or the exclusive agency system.

Directors and Officers Liability Insurance: Coverage for directors and officers of firms or organizations against liability claims arising out of alleged errors in judgment, breaches of duty, and wrongful acts related to their organizational activities.

Dividend: (1) An amount returned to a policyholder by an insurance company out of its earnings. (2) Also, in capital stock companies, a share of profits distributed to stockholders.

Domestic Insurance Company: In a given state, an insurer domiciled in that state.

Earned Premium: The portion of a premium which is the property of an insurance company, based on the expired portion of the policy period.

Embezzlement: Fraudulent use or taking of another's property or money which has been entrusted to one's care.

Employers Liability Coverage: A section of the workers' compensation policy which provides coverage against the common law liability of an employer for injuries to employees as distinguished from the liability imposed by a workers' compensation law.

Endorsement: A form attached to an insurance policy to add to, alter or vary its provisions.

Errors and Omissions Insurance: A form of insurance that indemnifies the insured for any loss sustained because of an error or oversight on his or her part.

Excess Limits: Coverage against losses in excess of a specified dollar limit.

Exclusion: A provision in an insurance policy which denies coverage for certain perils, persons, property, or locations.

Expense Ratio: The cost of acquiring, writing and servicing business as a percentage of written premiums.

Experience: The loss record of an insured or of a particular class of coverage.

Experience Rating: A method under which insurance rates are based on a policyholder's loss record.

Expiration Date: The date indicated in an insurance contract as its termination date.

Exposure: The state of being subject to the possibility of loss; the extent of risk as measured by various standards such as payroll, gate receipts and area.

Extended Coverage Insurance: Protection for the insured against property damage caused by windstorm, hail, smoke, explosion, riot, riot attending a strike, civil commotion, vehicle and aircraft. This is provided in conjunction with the fire insurance policy and the various "package" policies.

Facultative Reinsurance: A procedure by which insurance companies reinsure risks on an individual basis, with a reinsurer having the option to accept or decline each risk.

FAIR (Fair Access to Insurance Requirements) Plan: A facility, operating under a government-insurance industry cooperative program, to make fire insurance and other forms of property insurance readily available to persons who have difficulty obtaining such coverage.

Farmowners-Ranchowners Policy: A package policy for a farm or a ranch providing property and liability coverages against both personal and business losses.

Federal Crime Insurance: Insurance against burglary, larceny and robbery losses offered by the federal government where the Federal Insurance Administration has determined that such insurance is not otherwise readily available.

Fidelity Bond: A form of protection which reimburses an employer for losses caused by dishonest or fraudulent acts of employees.

Financial Responsibility Law: A law under which a person involved in an automobile accident may be required to furnish security up to certain minimum dollar limits.

Fire Insurance: Coverage for losses caused by fire, lightning and the removal of property from endangered premises, plus resultant damage caused by smoke and water.

Fleet Policy: A policy covering a number of motor vehicles (usually 5 or more) owned by a single insured.

Floater: A form of insurance that applies to movable property, whatever its location, within the territorial limits imposed by the contract. The coverage "floats" with the property.

Flood Insurance: Coverage against loss resulting from the flood peril.

Foreign Insurance Company: In a given state, an insurer domiciled in another state.

Fraud: Deception or strategy used to deceive or cheat, including misrepresentation or concealment.

General Average: In ocean marine insurance, a loss shared by all interests because of an expense or sacrifice voluntarily incurred to preserve all the property from destruction.

General Liability Insurance: Form of coverage that pertains, for the most part, to claims arising out of the insured's liability for injuries or damage caused by ownership of property, manufacturing operations, contracting operations, sale or distribution of products, and the operation of elevators and the like, as well as professional services.

Generally Accepted Accounting Principles (GAAP): A method of accounting used by insurance companies to produce results consistent with those of other industries.

Glass Insurance: Protection for loss of or damage to glass and its appurtenances.

Group Insurance: Any insurance plan under which a number of persons and their dependents are insured under a single policy, issued to their employer or to an association with which they are affiliated, with individual certificates given to each insured person.

Guaranty Fund: A fund, derived from assessments against solvent insurance companies, to absorb losses of claimants against insolvent insurers.

Hail Insurance: Coverage for loss or damage to growing crops due to hail.

Hazard: Condition which creates or increases the chances of a loss.

Health Insurance: Insurance against financial losses resulting from sickness or bodily injury.

Hold Harmless Agreement: A contract under which one party's legal liability for damages is assumed by the other party to the contract.

Homeowners Policy: A package type of insurance for the home owner that includes coverages ranging from fire and extended coverage, theft and personal liability to "all-risk" coverages.

Hull Policy: A contract that provides indemnification for damage to or loss of an insured vessel or airplane.

Hurricane: A tropical storm with a wind velocity of 75 or more miles an hour.

Indemnify: To provide financial compensation for losses.

Inland Marine Insurance: A broad type of insurance, generally covering articles that may be transported from one place to another as well as bridges, tunnels and other instrumentalities of transportation and communication. It includes goods in transit (generally excepting trans-ocean) as well as numerous "floater" policies such as those covering personal effects, personal property, jewelry, furs, fine arts and others.

Insurance: A system under which individuals, businesses and other organizations or entities, in exchange for payment of a sum of money (a premium), are guaranteed compensation for losses resulting from certain perils under specified conditions.

Insurance Contract: The agreement of an insurer to provide benefits or reimburse losses in return for a premium. A policy is the written statement of the insurance contract terms.

Insurance to Value: Insurance written in an amount approximating the value of the property insured.

Insuring Clause: That part of an insurance policy or bond which recites the agreement of the insurer to protect the insured against some form of loss or damage. Also known as Insuring Agreement.

Investment Income: The portion of a company's income which is derived from its investments, including interest and dividends earned on stocks and bonds.

Jettison: To throw overboard part of a ship's cargo in order to save the ship.

Joint Underwriting Association: An unincorporated association of insurance companies formed to provide a particular form of insurance to the public.

Judgment: An obligation created by the decree of a court.

Kidnap and Ransom Insurance: Insurance to cover the cost of ransom or extortion payments and related expenses.

Liability: Any legally enforceable obligation.

Liability Insurance: Insurance covering the policyholder's legal liability for injuries to other persons or damage to their property.

Life Insurance: Insurance providing for payment of a specified amount to an estate or a designated beneficiary on the death of the policyholder; or in the case of an endowment policy, to the policyholder at a specified date.

Limit: The maximum amount of benefits that an insurer agrees to pay in the event of a loss.

Line: A type or kind of insurance.

Lloyds: Groups of individuals, called syndicates (not insurance companies), assuming liability through an underwriter. Each individual independently and personally assumes a proportionate part of the risk accepted by the underwriter.

Loss: The basis on which an insurance claim is submitted and/or paid.

Loss Prevention Service: Engineering and inspection work done by an insurance company or independent organization with the aim of removing or reducing dangerous conditions in order to prevent losses.

Loss Ratio: The percentage of premiums (usually earned premiums) used to pay losses and loss adjustment expenses.

Loss Reserve: An insurer's estimated liability for unpaid insurance claims or losses that will have to be paid in the future.

Malicious Mischief: The willful damaging or destruction of another person's property.

Malpractice Insurance: See Professional Liability Insurance.

Manual: A book published by an insurance or bonding company, a rating association or bureau, giving rates, classifications and underwriting rules.

Manual Rates: Rates set forth in a manual.

Marine Insurance: A form of insurance primarily concerned with instruments of transportation and communication, and with goods in transit. See also Inland Marine Insurance and Ocean Marine Insurance.

Medical Payments Insurance: A coverage, available in various liability insurance policies, in which the insurer agrees to reimburse the insured and others, without regard for the insured's liability, for medical or funeral expenses incurred as the result of bodily injury or death by accident under specified conditions.

Multi-Peril Policy: A package policy which provides coverage against several different perils

Multiple-Line Policy: A multi-peril policy which combines both property and liability coverages.

Mutual Insurance Company: An incorporated insurance organization owned by its policyholders.

Mysterious Disappearance: The disappearance of property from a known place in a way that cannot be explained.

Named Insured: Any person, firm, or corporation designated in a policy as the insured(s).

Named Perils: Perils specified in a policy as those against which the policyholder is insured.

Nationwide Marine Definition: A statement of the types of insurance that may be written under marine or inland marine policies.

Negligence: Failure to use the degree of care which a person of reasonable prudence would use under given or similar circumstances. A person may be negligent by acts of omission or commission, or both.

Net Underwriting Profit or Loss: Statutory underwriting profit less (or loss plus) dividends to policyholders.

No-Fault Automobile Insurance: A form of insurance by which a person's financial losses resulting from an automobile accident, such as medical and hospital expenses and loss of income, are paid by his or her own insurance company without regard to fault.

Notice of Loss: A written notice to an insurance company from a person who has sustained a loss, giving notice to the company that the loss has occurred.

Obligee: A person, firm, corporation or government agency protected by a surety bond against loss.

Obligor: The party, sometimes called the principal, bound by obligation under a surety bond.

Occupational Disease: Sickness or disease arising out of or in the course of employment.

Ocean Marine Insurance: Coverage for sea-going vessels, including liabilities connected with them, and their cargoes.

Package Policy: A single insurance policy that includes several coverages.

Particular Average: In ocean marine insurance, a partial loss suffered by the insured without benefit of or right to renumeration from others. Contrast with General Average.

Peril: The cause of a loss insured against in a policy.

Personal Article Floater: A policy or an addition to another policy, used to cover personal valuables such as furs and jewelry.

Personal Lines: Those types of insurance, such as auto or home insurance, for individuals or families rather than for businesses or organizations.

Physical Damage: A term indicating actual damage to property.

Policy: A contract of insurance.

Policyholder: A person who pays a premium to an insurance company in exchange for the insurance protection provided by a policy of insurance.

Policyholders' Surplus: The sum remaining after all liabilities are deducted from all assets. Sums such as paid-in capital and special voluntary reserves are also included in this term. This surplus is an additional financial protection to policyholders in the event a company suffers unexpected or catastrophic losses. In effect, it is the financial base that permits a company to sell insurance.

Pool: An organization of insurers or reinsurers through which particular types of risk are underwritten with premiums, losses and expenses shared in agreed-upon amounts.

Premises: The particular location of property or a portion thereof as designated in a policy.

Premium: The sum paid for an insurance policy. **Net premiums written** represent premium income retained by insurance companies, direct or after reinsurance transactions. **Direct written premiums** are the amounts actually paid by policyholders.

Premium Discount: An amount subtracted from an insurance premium due to some merit or circumstance of the policyholder.

Principal: In suretyship, the individual or corporation whose performance is guaranteed.

Producer: A term applied to an agent, solicitor or other person who sells insurance.

Product Liability Insurance: Protection against financial loss arising out of the legal liability incurred by a manufacturer, merchant or distributor because of injury or damage resulting from the use of a covered product.

Professional Liability Insurance: Coverage for a professional practitioner, such as a doctor or a lawyer, against liability claims for damages resulting from alleged malpractice in the performance of the insured's services. Often called malpractice insurance.

Proof of Loss: A written statement made by the policyholder for the insurer regarding a claim so that the insurer may determine its liability under the policy or bond.

Property Damage Liability Insurance: Insurance against financial losses growing out of a policyholder's liability for damage to the property of another including loss of the use of the property.

Property Insurance: Insurance providing financial protection against the loss of, or damage to, real and personal property caused by specified perils.

Public Law 15: A federal statute (McCarran-Ferguson Act) passed in 1945 exempting the business of insurance from federal antitrust laws to the extent that insurance is regulated by the various states.

Public Liability Insurance: A general term applied to forms of both bodily injury and property damage liability. It protects the insured against claims brought by members of the public.

Rain Insurance: Insurance against loss of expected income or incurred expense when rain, hail, snow or sleet causes the cancellation of or reduced patronage at sales, fairs and similar events.

Rate: The cost of a given unit of insurance, on which a premium is based.

Rating Bureau: An organization, supported by insurers, which provides advisory, rating, statistical and other services relating to property and casualty insurance.

Rating Territory: A geographical subdivision of a state whose residents are grouped together for rating purposes.

Reciprocal Exchange: An unincorporated insuring organization comprising subscribers who insure each other.

Regulation: Supervision of business practices by a governmental entity.

Regulator: See Commissioner.

Reinsurance: Assumption by one insurance company of all or part of a risk undertaken by another insurance company.

Reinsurance Facility: A plan adopted in some states as an alternative to an automobile insurance plan. While each auto insurer serves its own policyholders, all participating companies pool their experience and share in the results on some equitable basis.

Renter's Policy: A homeowners policy adapted to the needs of people who rent. Also referred to as a tenants policy.

Replacement Cost: The cost of replacing property without a deduction for depreciation.

Representation: Statements made on an application for insurance reported by the applicant as being substantially true to the best of his or her knowledge or belief.

Reserve: (1) An amount representing actual or potential liabilities kept by an insurer to cover obligations to policyholders. (2) An amount allocated for a special purpose. Note that a reserve is usually a liability and not an extra fund. On occasion a reserve may be an asset, such as a reserve for taxes not yet due.

Retention: The amount of risk retained by an insurance company and not reinsured.

Retrospective Rating: A method permitting adjustment, subject to maximum and minimum limits, of the final premium for a risk on the basis of its own loss experience.

Rider: See Endorsement.

Risk: The chance of loss. Also used to refer to the insured or to property covered by a policy.

Risk Management: Management of the varied risks to which a business firm or corporation might be subject. It involves analyzing all exposures to gauge the possibility of loss and determining how to minimize losses by such means as insurance, reduction or elimination of risk or the practice of safety and security measures.

Robbery: The felonious taking, either by force or threat of force, of the property of another.

Safe Driver Plan: A merit rating program for private automobiles under which a car owner's driving record is used as a factor in determining the size of the premium.

Salvage: (1) Property taken over by an insurer, which has paid a claim, to reduce its loss; (2) to save endangered property and to enhance the value of damaged property; (3) in marine insurance, the cost of saving property exposed to a peril; (4) in suretyship, that which is recovered from the principal or an indemnitor to offset the loss and expense paid by a surety in satisfying its obligation under a bond.

Schedule: A list of individual items or groups of items covered under one policy.

Self-Insurance: An arrangement through which some firms and individuals plan to assume all or a portion of their own losses. Self-insurers often establish special funds for this purpose, and purchase insurance to cover losses in excess of predetermined amounts.

Solicitor: A person authorized by an agent to solicit and receive applications for insurance.

Special Multi-Peril Policy (SMP): A business policy which combines in one contract the coverages normally purchased under several policies. Many options and endorsements are available to tailor-make the policy to meet the needs of a policyholder.

State Fund: A fund set up by a state government to provide insurance. Some statutes permit, others exclude, competition by private insurers.

Statutory Accounting Principles (SAP): Statutory requirements which must be met by an insurance company when submitting its financial statement to the state insurance department.

Statutory Underwriting Profit or Loss: Premiums earned minus losses and expenses incurred.

Subrogation: The legal process by which an insurance company, after paying a loss, seeks to recover the amount of the loss from another who is legally liable for it.

Surety Bond: An agreement providing for monetary compensation should there be a failure to perform specific acts within a stated period. The surety company, for example, becomes responsible for fulfillment of a contract if the contractor defaults.

Suretyship: Obligations to pay the debts of, or answer for, the default of another.

Surplus Lines: (1) A risk or a part of a risk for which there is no normal insurance market available. (2) Insurance written by non-admitted insurance companies.

Syndicate: A group of insurers or underwriters who join to insure property that presents high values or high hazards. See also Pool.

Tenants Policy: See Renter's Policy.

Term: A period of time for which a policy is issued.

Theft: The act of stealing.

Third-Party: A person who files a liability insurance claim.

Title Insurance: Insurance which indemnifies the owner of real estate in the event that his or her clear ownership of property is challenged by the discovery of faults in the title.

Tornado: A whirling wind, accompanied by funnel-shaped cloud, very violent and destructive in a narrow path, often for many miles over the land.

Tort: A wrongful act, resulting in injury or damage, on which a civil action may be based. Does not apply to a breech of contract.

Treaty: A form of reinsurance agreement between insurance companies.

Treaty Reinsurance: A contract of reinsurance setting forth the conditions for reinsuring a class or classes of insurance.

Umbrella Liability: A form of insurance protection against losses in excess of the amount covered by other liability insurance policies; also protects the insured in many situations not covered by the usual liability policies.

Underinsurance: A condition in which not enough insurance is carried to cover the insurable value.

Underwriting: The process of selecting risks for insurance and determining in what amounts and on what terms the insurance company will accept the risk.

Underwriting Profit or Loss: The amount of money which an insurance company gains or loses as a result of its underwriting operations. A net gain or loss on underwriting operations represents a company's statutory underwriting result less any amount it may pay to its policyholders in the form of dividends.

Unearned Premium: The portion of a premium that a company has collected but has yet to earn because the policy still has unexpired time to run.

Uninsured Motorist Protection: A form of insurance which covers the policyholder and family members if injured by a hit-and-run motorist or a driver who carries no liability insurance, assuming the other driver is at fault.

Valued Policy: A policy under which an insurer agrees to pay a specified amount of money to or on behalf of the insured upon occurrence of a defined loss.

Vandalism: The malicious or ignorant, often random, destruction or spoilage of another person's property.

Void: A term used to describe a policy contract that for some reason specified in the policy becomes free of all legal effect.

Waiver: The surrender of a right or privilege which is known to exist.

Warranty: A statement made on an application for most kinds of insurance that is warranted as true in all respects. If untrue in any respect, even though the untruth was not known to the applicant, the contract may be voided without regard to the materiality of the statement.

Workers' Compensation Insurance: A method of providing for the cost of medical care and weekly payments to injured employees or to dependents of those killed in the workplace, regardless of blame.

Write: To insure, to underwrite, or to accept an application for insurance.

INSURANCE AND SERVICE ORGANIZATIONS

The following are among the national organizations of or supported by insurance companies, or whose activities are closely related to insurance.

AFIA World Wide Insurance, 110 William St., New York, N.Y. 10038—An organization representing a group of American capital stock insurance companies, it provides fire, marine, liability, accident and health, bonding and crime insurance and reinsurance to American and overseas business interests.

Alliance of American Insurers, 20 North Wacker Dr., Chicago, Ill. 60606—Trade association to facilitate cooperation among fire and casualty insurance companies in matters of concern to them and their policyholders.

All-Industry Research Advisory Council, 7315 Wisconsin Ave., Suite 231-W, Bethesda, Md. 20014—Provides the public and the insurance industry with timely research information relevant to public policy issues affecting risk and insurance.

American Association of Insurance Services, 221 N. LaSalle, Chicago, Ill. 60601—Rating, statistical and advisory organization for personal and commercial lines of insurance, with membership composed principally of small and medium size companies.

American Council of Life Insurance, 1850 K St., N.W., Washington, D.C. 20006—Trade association responsible for public relations, government, legislative and research aspects of the life insurance business.

American Institute of Marine Underwriters, 14 Wall Street, New York, N.Y. 10005—Provides information to marine underwriters, and promotes the interests of those underwriters.

American Institute for Property and Liability Underwriters, Inc., Providence and Sugartown Roads, Malvern, Pa. 19355—Establishes educational standards for professional property and liability insurance underwriting; fosters training.

American Insurance Association, 85 John Street, New York, N.Y. 10038—Trade and service organization of the property and casualty insurance industry; provides a forum for the discussion of problems; provides safety, promotional and legislative services.

American Nuclear Insurers, The Exchange, Building #3, Farmington Ave., Farmington, Conn. 06032—A non-profit, unincorporated association through which liability and property insurance protection is provided against hazards arising out of nuclear reactor installations and their operations.

Automobile Insurance Plans Service Office, 733 Third Avenue, New York, N.Y. 10017—Develops and files rates and provides other services for automobile insurance plans countrywide.

Casualty Actuarial Society, One Penn Plaza, New York, N.Y. 10001—Promotes actuarial and statistical science in all insurance fields except life.

College of Insurance, The, 123 William St., New York, N.Y. 10038—Insurance industry-supported college providing complete curricula leading to bachelor's and master's degrees in business administration and a bachelor of science degree in actuarial science.

Crop-Hail Insurance Actuarial Association, 209 W. Jackson Blvd., Chicago, Ill. 60606—Rating and research organization and statistical agent for crop-hail insurance and rain insurance on public events, business ventures, and private proceedings.

Factory Mutual System, 1151 Boston-Providence Turnpike, Norwood, Mass. 02062—Group of property insurance companies specializing in risks requiring a high degree of loss prevention. Also, provides loss prevention services.

Federal Insurance Administration, 451 Seventh St., S.W., Washington, D.C. 20410—Administers the federal flood insurance, urban property insurance and crime insurance programs.

Foreign Credit Insurance Association, One World Trade Center, 9th Flr., New York, N.Y. 10048—Offers credit insurance facilities for U.S. exporters through cooperation of the insurance business and the Export-Import Bank of Washington.

Health Insurance Institute, 1850 K Street, N.W., Washington, D.C. 20006—Central source of health insurance information for the public on behalf of insurance companies; monitors public attitudes and reactions to health insurance developments.

Highway Loss Data Institute, Watergate Six Hundred, 600 New Hampshire Ave., N.W., Washington, D.C. 20037—Non-profit organization to gather, process and provide the public with insurance data concerned with human and economic losses resulting from highway accidents.

Independent Insurance Agents of America, Inc., 85 John St., New York, N.Y. 10038—Trade association of independent insurance agents.

Industrial Risk Insurers, 85 Woodland St., Hartford, Conn. 06102—An engineering, research, and underwriting association composed of more than 40 insurance companies. Provides specialized insurance and advisory fire protection services for risks requiring a high degree of loss control in the U.S. and Puerto Rico and U.S. companies domiciled overseas.

Inland Marine Underwriters Association, 14 Wall St., New York, N.Y. 10005—Forum for discussion of problems of common concern to inland marine insurers; makes recommendations dealing with policy forms and legislation.

Institute for Civil Justice, 1700 Main St., Santa Monica, Calif. 90406—Organization formed within the Rand Corporation to perform independent, objective research and analysis concerning the civil justice system.

Insurance Accounting and Statistical Association, Mutual Plaza, Durham, N.C. 27701—An international organization to promote the study, research and development of modern techniques in insurance accounting and statistics.

Insurance Arbitration Forums, 83 Maiden Lane, New York, N.Y. 10038—Industry-supported, non-profit organization to arbitrate inter-company disputes.

Insurance Company Education Directors Society, % State Automobile Mutual Insurance Company, 518 East Broad St., Columbus, Ohio 43216—Professional society of company education directors and others involved in insurance-related educational activities.

Insurance Crime Prevention Institute, 15 Franklin St., Westport, Conn. 06880—Serves insurers in the investigation of fradulent insurance claims, other than workers' compensation, accident and health insurance.

Insurance Information Institute, 110 William St., New York, N.Y. 10038—An educational, fact-finding and communications organization for all lines of insurance except life and health insurance. It is supported by more than 200 insurance companies and provides services on a subscribership basis to many major industry organizations.

Insurance Institute for Highway Safety, Watergate Six Hundred, 600 New Hampshire Ave., N.W., Washington, D.C. 20037—Traffic safety organization supported by automobile insurers.

Insurance Institute for Research, 222 Mamaroneck Ave., White Plains, N.Y. 10605—An industry-sponsored institute serving as the focal point for improving electronic communications capabilities in the insurance agency system.

Insurance Institute of America, Inc., Providence and Sugartown Roads, Malvern, Pa. 19355—Provides educational opportunities in property and liability insurance and related fields; provides standards for measurement of achievement; conducts research.

Insurance Services Office, 160 Water St., New York, N.Y. 10038—Provides a wide range of advisory, rating, actuarial, statistical and other services relating to property and casualty insurance, including the development of policy forms, rates, premiums and related services for multiple-line coverages. Offers services, including research studies, to insurers or other persons or organizations.

Mutual Atomic Energy Liability Underwriters, One East Wacker Dr., Chicago, Ill. 60601—An underwriting syndicate of six mutual casualty insurance companies which writes the primary policies of nuclear energy liability insurance.

Mutual Atomic Energy Reinsurance Pool, One East Wacker Dr., Chicago, Ill. 60601—104 companies providing reinsurance capacity for atomic energy reinsurance contracts underwritten by American Mutual Reinsurance Co.

National Association of Independent Insurers, 2600 River Rd., Des Plaines, Ill. 60018—Trade association of fire, casualty and surety insurers.

National Association of Insurance Brokers, Inc., 311 1st St., N.W., Washington, D.C. 20001—Trade association of commercial insurance brokers.

National Association of Insurance Commissioners, 350 Bishops Way, Brookfield (Milwaukee), Wis. 53005—Organization of state insurance commissioners to promote uniformity in state supervision of insurance matters, and to recommend desirable legislation in the various state legislatures.

National Association of Mutual Insurance Companies, 7931 Castleway Dr., Indianapolis, Ind. 46250—Trade association of mutual property and casualty insurance companies.

National Association of Surety Bond Producers, Inc., 5225 Wisconsin Ave., N.W., Suite 502, Washington, D.C. 20015—Trade association of surety bond producers.

National Automobile Theft Bureau, 10330 S. Roberts Rd., Palos Hills, Ill. 60482—Conducts stolen vehicle recovery and auto theft prevention activities on behalf of the insurance industry.

National Committee on Insurance Guaranty Funds, 85 John St., New York, N.Y. 10038—Advisory organization to the state guaranty fund boards; gathers and disseminates information regarding insurer insolvencies.

National Committee on Property Insurance, City Bank & Trust Building, 55 Court St., Suite 210, Boston, Mass. 02108—A national organization of insurers which is concerned with operations of residual property insurance markets.

National Council on Compensation Insurance, One Penn Plaza, New York, N.Y. 10001—Develops and administers rating plans and systems for workers' compensation insurance.

National Crime Prevention Association, 985 National Press Bldg., 529 14th St., N.W., Washington, D.C. 20045—Coordinates national strategy and provides information on crime prevention efforts.

National Crop Insurance Association, 2860 S. Circle Dr., Building 1, Suite 322, Colorado Springs, Colo. 80906—National trade association of insurance companies writing hail, fire and other weather perils to growing crops.

National Fire Protection Association, 470 Atlantic Ave., Boston, Mass. 02210—Independent, non-profit source of technical and educational information on fire protection, prevention and suppression; develops and publishes consensus fire safety standards; sponsors national Learn Not to Burn campaign.

National Safety Council, 444 North Michigan Ave., Chicago, Ill. 60611—Provides national support and leadership in the field of safety; publishes safety materials of all kinds; conducts a public information and publicity program in support of safety.

New York Insurance Exchange, 59 John St., New York, N.Y. 10038—A facility for the underwriting of reinsurance of all kinds, direct insurance of all kinds on risks located entirely outside the U.S., and direct insurance on risks which have been rejected in the New York Free Trade Zone.

Overseas Private Investment Corporation, 1129 20th St., N.W., Washington, D.C. 20527—Administers the U.S. government political risk insurance and finance programs designed to encourage private investment in developing countries.

Professional Insurance Agents, 400 N. Washington St., Alexandria, Va. 22314—Trade association of insurance agents.

Property-Casualty Insurance Council, 1st National Bank Plaza, Suite 3950, Chicago, Ill. 60603—Organization of property and casualty insurance associations and companies to provide a forum for discussion of major issues and to facilitate coordination and cooperation in dealing with those issues, and to develop and recommend programs in research and in consumer and legislative information.

Property Insurance Plans Service Office, City Bank & Trust Bldg., 55 Court St., Suite 210, Boston, Mass. 02108—Provides technical and administrative services to state property insurance plans.

Reinsurance Association of America, 1025 Connecticut Ave., N.W., Suite 512, Washington, D.C. 20036—Trade association of property and casualty reinsurers; provides legislative services for members.

Risk and Insurance Management Society, Inc., 205 E. 42nd St., New York, N.Y. 10017—Organization of corporate buyers of insurance, which advises insurers of the needs of business and industry, supports loss prevention and provides a forum for the discussion of common objectives and problems.

Society of Certified Insurance Counselors, 3630-C North Hills Dr., Austin, Tex. 78731—A national education and designation program in the fields of property, liability and life insurance with a continuing education requirement upon designation.

Society of Chartered Property and Casualty Underwriters, Kahler Hall, Providence Rd. (CB No. 9), Malvern, Pa. 19355—Professional society to foster the higher education of those engaged in insurance and risk management; encourages and conducts research.

Surety Association of America, 100 Wood Ave. South (Metro-Park), Iselin, N.J. 08830—Statistical, rating, development and advisory organization and forum for surety companies.

Underwriters' Laboratories, Inc., 207 E. Ohio St., Chicago, Ill. 60611—Investigates and tests electrical materials and other products to determine that fire prevention and protection standards are being met.

Underwriters' Salvage Company, 1400 Busse Road, Elk Grove Village, Ill. 60007—Makes appraisals and disposition of damaged, distressed, close-out and bankruptcy merchandise for the benefit of insurance companies and/or general commerce.

RELATED PUBLICATIONS

There are many textbooks, periodicals and other reference works which deal with the subject of property/casualty insurance. The following is a selective listing of such reference materials.

STANDARD REFERENCE WORKS

Best's Aggregates & Averages, Property-Casualty, A.M. Best Company, Oldwick, N.J. 08858—annual

Gives figures by companies and by aggregates for stock, mutual, reciprocal and Lloyds organizations.

Best's Insurance Reports, Property-Casualty, A.M. Best Company, Oldwick, N.J. 08858—annual

Reports on and rates the financial position, history and transactions of insurers in the United States and Canada.

Books In Insurance, Insurance Information Institute, 110 William St., New York, N.Y. 10038—updated periodically

A selective listing of books, including textbooks, and periodicals about insurance.

Fire, Casualty & Surety Bulletins, The National Underwriter Company, 420 E. Fourth St., Cincinnati, Ohio 45202—loose-leaf

Five volumes on Fire & Marine, Casualty & Surety, Companies & Coverages, Personal Lines, and Management & Sales which form a reference to all aspects of P/C coverages.

The Insurance Almanac, The Underwriter Printing and Publishing Company, 50 East Palisade Ave., Englewood, N.J. 07631—annual

Lists of and information concerning state insurance officials, national and state insurance organizations, companies. Also a limited geographical listing of adjusters, agents and brokers.

Insurance Facts: Property, Liability, Marine, Surety, Insurance Information Institute, 110 William St., New York, N.Y. 10038—annual

A yearbook giving selected data of general interest relating to property/casualty insurance.

General Insurance Guide, Werbel Publishing Company, 595 Old Willets Path, Smithtown, N.Y. 11787—loose-leaf

A three volume reference source providing information relating to all coverages.

OTHER PERIODICALS

American Agent and Broker, Commerce Publishing Co., 408 Olive St., St. Louis, Mo. 63102—monthly
Best's Review, Property/Casualty Insurance Edition, A.M. Best Co., Oldwick, N.J. 08858—monthly
Business Insurance, 740 Rush St., Chicago, Ill. 60611—bi-weekly
CPCU Journal, The Society of Chartered Property and Casualty Underwriters, Kahler Hall, Providence Rd. (CB#9), Malvern, Penn. 19355—quarterly
Independent Agent, Independent Insurance Agents of America, Inc., 85 John St., New York, N.Y. 10038—monthly
Insurance Adjuster, Insurance Adjuster, Inc., 2322 Seattle First National Bank Bldg., Seattle, Wash. 98154—monthly
Insurance Advocate, Roberts Publishing Corp., 45 John St., New York, N.Y. 10038—weekly
The Insurance Journal, The Insurance Journal, Inc., 34-35 Wilshire, Suite 1610, Los Angeles, Calif. 90010—semiweekly
Insurance Marketing, Bayard Publications, 1243 Summer St., Stamford, Conn. 06905—monthly
Insurance Record, Record Publications, Inc., P.O. Box 225770, Dallas, Tex. 75265—26 times a year
Insuranceweek, Insuranceweek, Inc., 2322 Seattle First National Bank Bldg., Seattle, Wash. 98154—weekly
International Insurance Monitor, International Insurance Monitor, 150 W. 28th St., New York, N.Y. 10001—monthly
Journal of American Insurance, Alliance of American Insurers, 20 N. Wacker Dr., Chicago, Ill. 60606—quarterly
The Journal of Insurance, Insurance Information Institute, 110 William St., New York, N.Y. 10038—bi-monthly
Journal of Risk & Insurance, American Risk and Insurance Association, Brooks Hall, Univ. of Georgia, Athens, Ga. 30602—quarterly
Mid-America Insurance, William S. Howard Co., 3742 Broadway, Suite 201, Kansas City, Mo. 64111—monthly
National Underwriter, Property/Casualty Insurance Edition, The National Underwriter Co., 420 E. 4th St., Cincinnati, Ohio 45202—weekly
The Pro-Agent, Professional Insurance Agents, 400 N. Washington St., Alexandria, Va. 22314—monthly
Risk Management, Risk and Insurance Management Society, Inc., 205 E. 42nd St., New York, N.Y. 10017—monthly
Rough Notes, The Rough Notes Co., Inc., 1200 N. Meridian St., Indianapolis, Ind. 46206—monthly
Southern Insurance, Southern Insurance, 704 Cigali Bldg., 107 Camp St., New Orleans, La. 70130—monthly
The Standard, The Standard Publishing Co., 89 Broad St., Boston, Mass. 02110—weekly
Today's Insurance Woman, National Association of Insurance Women (International), 1847 East 15th St., P.O. Box 4694, Tulsa, Okla. 74104—quarterly
Underwriters' Report, Underwriters' Report of California, 667 Mission St., San Francisco, Calif. 94105—weekly
United States Banker, Cleworth Publishing Co., Inc., One River Rd., Cos Cob, Conn. 06807—monthly

Weekly Underwriter, Underwriter Printing & Publishing Co., 50 E. Palisade Ave., Englewood, N.J. 07631—weekly

Western Underwriter, Farwest Insurance Press, 1215 Second St., P.O. Box 856, San Rafael, Calif. 94902—semimonthly

SELECTED TEXTS

General Insurance, 10th Edition—1979. David I. Bickelhaupt. Richard D. Irwin, Inc., 1818 Ridge Rd., Homewood, Ill. 60430.

Standard college text, presenting basic concepts followed by discussions of various lines: fire, marine, casualty, surety.

Insurance Principles and Practices—1980. Frederick G. Crane. John Wiley and Sons, Inc., 605 Third Ave., New York, N.Y. 10016.

Introductory text covering the fundamentals of insurance.

Principles of Insurance, 7th Edition—1980. Robert I. Mehr and Emerson Cammack. Richard D. Irwin, Inc., 1818 Ridge Rd., Homewood, Ill. 60430.

Basic principles for anyone interested in a broad knowledge of insurance as an economic and business institution.

Risk and Insurance, 5th Edition—1981. Mark R. Greene and James S. Trieschmann. South-Western Pub. Co., 5101 Madison Rd., Cincinnati, Ohio 45227.

Text which covers the basic ideas, problems and principles found in all types of modern day insurance, as well as other methods of handling risk.

MEMBER COMPANIES INSURANCE INFORMATION INSTITUTE

Aetna Life & Casualty
- The Aetna Casualty and Surety Company
- Aetna Casualty & Surety Company of America
- Aetna Casualty & Surety Company of Illinois
- The Automobile Insurance Company of Hartford, Connecticut
- The Standard Fire Insurance Company

Allianz Insurance Company

Allstate Insurance Companies
- Allstate Insurance Company
- Allstate Indemnity Company
- Northbrook Excess and Surplus Insurance Company
- Northbrook Indemnity Company
- Northbrook National Insurance Company
- Northbrook Property and Casualty Insurance Company

American Credit Indemnity Company of New York

American Re-Insurance Companies
- American Excess Insurance Company
- American Re-Insurance Company

The American Star Insurance Company

American Universal Companies
- American Universal Insurance Company
- Canadian Universal Insurance Company, Incorporated
- Canadian Universal Insurance Company, Limited

The Atlantic Companies
- Atlantic Mutual Insurance Company
- Centennial Insurance Company

Atlantic Mutual Fire Insurance Company

Attleboro Mutual Fire Insurance Company

Bituminous Insurance Companies
- Bituminous Casualty Corporation
- Bituminous Fire and Marine Insurance Company

CG/Aetna Insurance Company
- Aetna Fire Underwriters Insurance Company
- Aetna Insurance Company
- Aetna Insurance Company of the Midwest
- Century Indemnity Company

Cherokee Insurance Company

Chubb Group of Insurance Companies
- Alliance Assurance Company, Ltd.
- Chubb Lloyds Insurance Company of Texas
- Federal Insurance Company
- Great Northern Insurance Company
- The London Assurance
- Northwestern Pacific Indemnity Company
- Pacific Indemnity Company
- The Sea Insurance Company, Limited
- The Sumitomo Marine & Fire Insurance Company, Limited
- Sun Insurance Office Limited
- Texas Pacific Indemnity Company
- Vigilant Insurance Company

Commercial Union Insurance Companies
- American Employers' Insurance Company
- Bishop Insurance of Hawaii, Inc.
- Commercial Union Insurance Company
- Commercial Union Surplus Lines Insurance Company
- The Employers' Fire Insurance Company
- The Northern Assurance Company of America

The Continental Insurance Companies
- Boston Old Colony Insurance Company
- The Buckeye Union Insurance Company
- Commercial Insurance Company of Newark, New Jersey
- The Continental Insurance Company
- Continental Reinsurance Corporation
- Equitable Fire Insurance Company
- The Fidelity & Casualty Company of New York
- Firemen's Insurance Company of Newark, New Jersey
- First Insurance Company of Hawaii, Ltd.
- The Glens Falls Insurance Company
- Kansas City Fire & Marine Insurance Company
- London Guarantee & Accident Company of New York
- National-Ben Franklin Insurance Company of Illinois
- National-Ben Franklin Insurance Company of Michigan

Phoenix Assurance Company of New York
Niagara Fire Insurance Company

Crum and Forster Companies

U.S. Insurance Group

International Insurance Company
The North River Insurance Company
United States Fire Insurance Company
Westchester Fire Insurance Company

Industrial Indemnity Companies

Industrial Indemnity Company
Industrial Indemnity Company of Alaska
Industrial Indemnity of the Northwest
Industrial Insurance Company
Industrial Insurance Company of Hawaii, Ltd.
Industrial Underwriters Insurance Company

Cumis Insurance Society, Inc.

Employers Reinsurance Corporation

Excelsior Insurance Company of New York

Fireman's Fund Insurance Companies

American Automobile Insurance Company
The American Insurance Company
Associated Indemnity Corporation
Fireman's Fund Insurance Company
Fireman's Fund Insurance Company of Texas
National Surety Corporation
National Surety Corporation of California
San Francisco Insurance Company

Foundation Reserve Companies

Foundation Reserve Insurance Company, Inc.
Lloyds of New Mexico Insurance Company

General Accident Group

The Camden Fire Insurance Association
General Accident Fire & Life Assurance Corporation, Ltd.
Pennsylvania General Insurance Company
Potomac Insurance Company

General Reinsurance Group

General Reinsurance Corporation
North Star Reinsurance Corporation

The Harford Mutual Insurance Company

The Hartford Insurance Group

Hartford Accident and Indemnity Company
Hartford Casualty Insurance Company
Hartford Fire Insurance Company
New York Underwriters Insurance Company
Pacific Insurance Company, Ltd.
Sentinel Insurance Company, Ltd.
Twin City Fire Insurance Company

The Hartford Steam Boiler Inspection and Insurance Company

Hochheim Companies

Hochheim Prairie Casualty Insurance Company
Hochheim Prairie Farm Mutual Insurance Association

Home Insurance Companies

City Insurance Company
The Home Indemnity Company
The Home Insurance Company
The Home Insurance Company of Illinois
The Home Insurance Company of Indiana

INA Companies

Alaska Pacific Assurance Company
Allied Insurance Company
Bankers Standard Fire and Marine Company
Bankers Standard Insurance Company
Illinois Union Insurance Company
INA Insurance Company of Illinois
INA Insurance Company of Ohio
INA of Texas
INA Underwriters Insurance Company
Indemnity Insurance Company of North America
Insurance Company of North America
Pacific Employers Insurance Company

Kemper Group

American Manufacturers Mutual Insurance Company
American Motorists Insurance Company
American Protection Insurance Company
Economy Fire & Casualty Company
Economy Preferred Insurance Company
Federal Kemper Insurance Company
Iowa Kemper Insurance Company
Kemper County Mutual Insurance Company of Dallas
Kemper Security Insurance Company
Lumbermens Mutual Casualty Company
National Auto and Casualty Insurance Company
Sequoia Insurance Company

The Maryland

American General Fire and Casualty Company
American General Insurance Company
American General Lloyds
Assurance Company of America
Maine Bonding and Casualty Company
Maryland Casualty Company
National Standard Insurance Company
Northern Insurance Company of New York
Steadfast Insurance Company
Valiant Insurance Company

Merchants Insurance Group

Merchants Insurance Company of New Hampshire, Inc.
Merchants Mutual Insurance Company

The Merchants Property Insurance Company of Indiana

Millers National-Illinois Group

Illinois Insurance Company
Millers National Insurance Company

Montgomery Ward Insurance Group

Forum Insurance Company
Montgomery Ward Insurance Company

Munich American Reinsurance Group

Munich American Reinsurance Company
Munich Reinsurance Company

Nationwide Insurance Companies

Nationwide General Insurance Company
Nationwide Mutual Fire Insurance Company
Nationwide Mutual Insurance Company
Nationwide Property and Casualty Insurance Company

North American Reinsurance Group

North American Reinsurance Corporation
Swiss Reinsurance Company—U.S. Branch

Pennsylvania National Mutual Casualty Insurance Company

Ranger Insurance

Ranger County Mutual Insurance Company
Ranger Insurance Company
Ranger Lloyds

The Reinsurance Corporation of New York

Reliance Insurance Companies

General Casualty Company of Illinois
General Casualty Company of Wisconsin
Planet Insurance Company
Regent Insurance Company
Reliance Insurance Company
Reliance Insurance Company of Illinois
Reliance Insurance Company of New York
Reliance Lloyds

United Pacific Insurance Company
United Pacific Insurance Company of New York

Republic Insurance Group
Blue Ridge Insurance Company
Home Owners Insurance Company
Republic Insurance Company
Republic Underwriters Insurance Company
Republic-Vanguard Insurance Company
Vanguard Insurance Company
Vanguard Underwriters Insurance Company

Royal Insurance
American and Foreign Insurance Company
Globe Indemnity Company
Newark Insurance Company
Royal Indemnity Company
Royal Insurance Company of America
Safeguard Insurance Company

Rumford Property and Liability Insurance Company

Safeco Insurance Companies
First National Insurance Company of America
General Insurance Company of America
Safeco Insurance Company of America
Safeco National Insurance Company

The St. Paul
St. Paul Fire & Marine Insurance Company
St. Paul Guardian Insurance Company
The St. Paul Insurance Company
The St. Paul Insurance Company of Illinois
St. Paul Mercury Insurance Company
St. Paul Surplus Lines Insurance Company

Scor Reinsurance Company

Seaboard Surety Company

Security Insurance Group
The Connecticut Indemnity Company
The Fire & Casualty Insurance Company of Connecticut
Security Insurance Company of Hartford

Selected Risks Group
Selected Risks Insurance Company
Select Way Insurance Company

Skandia Group
American European Reinsurance Corporation
Hudson Insurance Company
Skandia America Reinsurance Corporation

The Travelers Insurance Companies
The Charter Oak Fire Insurance Company
The Phoenix Insurance Company
The Travelers Indemnity Company
The Travelers Indemnity Company of America
The Travelers Indemnity Company of Illinois
The Travelers Indemnity Company of Rhode Island
The Travelers Insurance Company

Trenwick Reinsurance Company, Ltd. (Associate Member)

United States Fidelity and Guaranty Company

Utica National Insurance Group
Graphic Arts Mutual Insurance Company
Utica Mutual Insurance Company

The Western Insurance Companies
The Western Casualty and Surety Company
The Western Fire Insurance Company
The Western Indemnity Company, Inc.

OFFICES OF THE INSURANCE INFORMATION INSTITUTE

HOME OFFICE

110 William Street, New York, N.Y. 10038
Tel. (212) 669-9200

FIELD OFFICES

Central-Southwestern Region

Traders National Bank Building, 1125 Grand Avenue, Suite 1125
Kansas City, Missouri 64106
Tel. (816) 421-0100

Eastern Region

110 William Street, New York, N.Y. 10038
Tel. (212) 669-9200

Midwestern Region

175 West Jackson Boulevard, Chicago, Illinois 60604
Tel. (312) 922-5584

Lansing Office

Suite 715, 109 W. Michigan Avenue, Lansing, Michigan 48933
Tel. (517) 372-4855

New England Region

27 School Street, Suite 305, Boston, Mass. 02108
Tel. (617) 227-8877

Northwestern Region

1218 Third Avenue, Seattle, Washington 98101
Tel. (206) 624-3330

Pacific Coast Region

400 Montgomery Street, San Francisco, California 94104
Tel. (415) 392-3185

South Central Region

Ten-O-One Building, 1001 Howard Avenue, Suite 2303,
New Orleans, Louisiana 70113
Tel. (504) 566-0540

Southeastern Region

6 Executive Park Drive, N.E., Suite 270, Atlanta, Georgia 30329
Tel. (404) 321-4615

Texas Region

1011 Congress Avenue, Suite 501, Austin, Texas 78701
Tel. (512) 476-7025

Dallas Office

1509 Main Street, Suite 1022, Dallas, Texas 75201
Tel. (214) 741-5195

Washington, D.C. Office

Suite 370, 1025 Vermont Avenue, N.W., Washington, D.C. 20005
Tel. (202) 347-3929

INDEX

A

B

C

D

E

F

J

K

L

M

Q

R

S

T

U

V

W

Y